Kingfisher
Science
Encyclopedia

General Editor: Catherine Headlam

10

ULTRA HIGH FREQUENCY ● ZYGOTE

Kingfisher

KINGFISHER
an imprint of Larousse plc
Elsley House, 24–30 Great Titchfield Street
London W1P 7AD

First published by Kingfisher 1991
Reprinted 1993, 1995 (with revisions) (twice), 1997

British Library Cataloguing-in-Publication Data
A catalogue record for this book is available from the British Library

ISBN 1 85697 456 1

Typesetting: Tradespools Ltd, Frome,
Somerset
Printed in Spain

GENERAL EDITOR
Catherine Headlam

EDITORIAL DIRECTOR
Jim Miles

ASSISTANT EDITORS
Lee Simmons
Charlotte Evans

EDITORIAL ASSISTANT
Andrea Moran

CONSULTANTS
Professor Lawrence F. Lowery, University of California, Berkeley, USA
Alison Porter, Education Officer, Science Museum, London

EDUCATIONAL CONSULTANTS
Terry Cash, Coordinator of a team of advisory teachers in Essex
Robert Pressling, Maths Coordinator,
Hillsgrove Primary School, London

CONTRIBUTORS
Joan Angelbeck
Michael Chinery
John Clark
Neil Curtis
Gwen Edmonds
Andrew Fisher
William Gould
Ian Graham
William Hemsley
James Muirden
John Paton
Brian Ward
Wendy Wasels
Peter Way

DESIGN
Ralph Pitchford
Allan Hardcastle
Ross George
Judy Crammond

PICTURE RESEARCH
Tim Russell
Elaine Willis

PRODUCTION
Dawn Hickman

SAFETY CODE

Some science experiments can be dangerous. Ask an adult to help you with difficult hammering or cutting and any experiments that involve flames, hot liquids or chemicals. Do not forget to put out any flames and turn off the heat when you have finished. Good scientists avoid accidents.

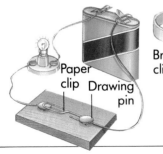

Paper clip
Drawing pin

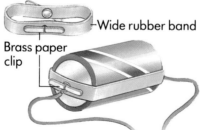

Wide rubber band
Brass paper clip

ELECTRICITY
- Never use mains electricity for experiments.
- Use batteries for all experiments that need electricity. Dispose of batteries carefully when they are used up and never heat them up or take them apart.

HEATING
- Tie back hair and be careful of loose clothes.
- Only heat small quantities of a substance.
- Always have an adult with you.
- Never heat any container with a top on it. Always point what you are heating away from you.
- Never hold something in your hands to heat it. Use a holder that does not conduct heat.

SAFE SOURCES OF HEAT
- Hot water from the tap or kettle is a good source of heat.
- A hair dryer can be used to dry things. Always take care when using electricity near water.

- For direct heat use a night light or short thick candle placed in sand in a metal tray.

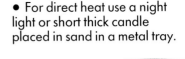

Sand
Metal tray

CHEMICALS AND QUANTITIES
- Only use a small amount of any substance even if it is just salt or vinegar.
- Never taste or eat chemicals
- Clean up all spillages immediately, especially if on your skin.
- Wash your hands after using chemicals.
- Always ask an adult before using any substance; many cooking or cleaning substances used at home are quite powerful.
- Smell chemicals very carefully. Do not breathe in deeply any strong smells.
- Never handle chemicals with your bare hands. Use an old spoon and wash it very carefully after use.
- Label **all** chemicals.

SUN
- Never look directly at the Sun, especially when using a telescope or binoculars.

PLANTS AND ANIMALS
- Never pick wild flowers.
- Collect insects carefully so as not to harm them. Release them afterwards.
- Be careful of stinging insects.

SAFE CONTAINERS
- Use plastic containers if an experiment does not require heating or strong chemicals.
- Use heat-proof glass or metal containers if you are using heat.
- Avoid using ordinary glass as it may shatter.

CUTTING
- Use scissors rather than a knife whenever possible.
- When using a knife keep your fingers behind the cutting edge.
- Put what you are cutting on a board that will not slip and will prevent damage to the surface underneath.

Ultra high frequency (UHF)

Ultra high frequency (UHF) is the name given to ELEC-TROMAGNETIC RADIATION which has an even higher FREQUENCY than VERY HIGH FREQUENCY (VHF) radio waves. A UHF wave has a frequency between 300 and 3000 MHz (a MHz is one million cycles per second). Because of its frequency, a UHF radio wave can carry much more information every second than an ordinary radio wave or a VHF signal. For example, UHF radio waves are used to broadcast TELEVISION signals. These involve a great deal of information because one of three colours has to be given to each spot on the screen each time the beam of the CATHODE RAY TUBE in the television set passes over it. Hundreds of thousands of spots are scanned 25 or 30 times every second, so tens of millions of pieces of information have to be carried every second.

UHF signals are used to communicate with artificial SATELLITES and other spacecraft. Again they allow a lot of information to be transferred and they can pass easily through the IONOSPHERE, the layer of the upper ATMOSPHERE that reflects ordinary radio waves.

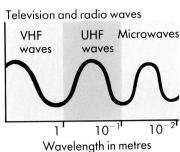

Television and radio waves

VHF waves | UHF waves | Microwaves

1   10^{-1} 10^{-2}
Wavelength in metres

▲ Ultra high frequency waves have frequencies greater than very high frequency waves but lower than microwaves.

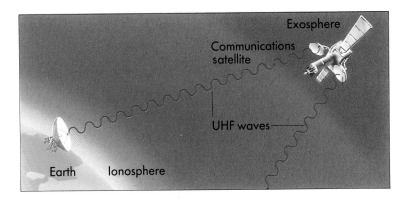

Exosphere
Communications satellite
UHF waves
Earth   Ionosphere

◄ UHF waves travel in straight lines and pass through all the layers of the Earth's atmosphere without being bent or reflected (unlike radio waves of lower frequencies). They are used to send telephone messages, television signals and computer data over long distances via communications satellites.

Ultrasound

Ultrasound is SOUND that cannot be heard because its FREQUENCY is greater than the highest frequency that the human EAR can detect. Sound with a frequency greater than 20 kHz (a kHz is one thousand cycles per second) can be described as ultrasound or ultrasonic. Ultrasound has a wide variety of uses. If the sound vibrations are strong enough, they can shake objects clean. If a dirty object is dipped into water and the ultrasound is switched on, the dirt is vibrated loose and falls from the object. The vibrations can also be used to break up

An ultrasonic wave passed through a liquid or a solid makes the liquid or solid vibrate at a very fast rate. These vibrations can be used to mix paint thoroughly, clean tools and homogenize milk by breaking up the fat particles. In dentistry, a drill controlled by ultrasonic vibrations can penetrate tooth enamel with very little friction or heat.

▶ *An ultrasound scanner builds up a picture of an unborn baby in its mother's womb. This technique, which is painless for the mother and harmless for the baby, is used to check the progress of pregnancy.*

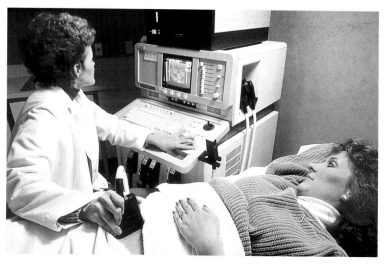

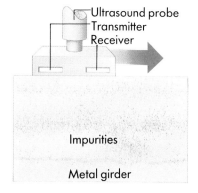

Ultrasound probe
Transmitter
Receiver

Impurities

Metal girder

▲ *Ultrasound scanning is used to detect flaws and impurities in metals. The ultrasound probe is moved along the surface of the metal to be tested. The probe has a transmitter to produce ultrasound and a receiver to detect it. The main reflections, or echoes, come from the top and bottom surfaces. But any impurities also reflect the ultrasonic waves and show up as a trace on a screen or print out.*

▶ *The eyes of some insects, such as bees, are sensitive to ultraviolet light. To a bee, these lobelia flowers look dark with pale lines down the middle of the petals. This encourages it to visit the flowers and pollinate them. Humans cannot see these lines* (right) *because in visible light the petals appear pale all over.*

painful growths in the kidneys called kidney stones.

Ultrasound can be used to reveal details that cannot normally be seen. Ships and submarines have SONAR systems that use ultrasound to 'see' under water. Scanners used in hospitals to check on the progress of unborn babies also use ultrasound. A scanner transmits ultrasound into the mother's body and receives reflections from inside. The reflections are displayed as a picture on a screen. Ultrasound is used because it is safer for the developing baby than X-rays.

Ultraviolet radiation

Ultraviolet radiation is ELECTROMAGNETIC RADIATION which has a higher FREQUENCY than the LIGHT we can see. It lies beyond the blue or violet end of the visible SPECTRUM. Each PHOTON (particle) of ultraviolet light carries more ENERGY than photons of visible light, so

MOLECULES which absorb ultraviolet radiation receive a large amount of energy. This extra energy can cause the molecule to break apart. This means that CHEMICAL REACTIONS can take place in ultraviolet light which would not otherwise occur. Ultraviolet light in sunlight can cause people's skin to burn. Large amounts of ultraviolet radiation can be dangerous. The OZONE LAYER is important because it absorbs most of the ultraviolet radiation from the Sun before it reaches the Earth.
See also INFRARED RADIATION; PHOTOCHEMISTRY.

Universe

The Universe is the whole of space and everything in it. Astronomers believe that it was formed after the BIG BANG, which probably took place about 15,000 million years ago. It has been expanding ever since, and the clusters of GALAXIES in it (including the cluster containing the MILKY WAY, where our SOLAR SYSTEM is located), are flying further apart. Although the Universe is getting larger, this does not mean that it has an 'edge' like an expanding balloon. This is because the force of GRAVITY in the space between the clusters of galaxies makes anything travelling through it follow a curved path, even though it seems to be straight. Trying to find the edge of

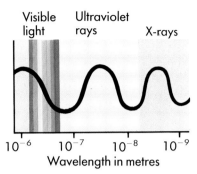

▲ Ultraviolet rays have shorter wavelengths than visible light and lie beyond the violet end of the spectrum. (10^{-6} metres is one thousandth of a millimetre.)

Edwin Hubble (1889–1953)
Hubble was an American astronomer whose work provided evidence for the theory that the Universe is expanding. In the 1920s he studied hundreds of distant galaxies and, by measuring the red shift in their spectra, showed that they are moving rapidly away from each other. He also classified galaxies into various types.

◄ The Universe is made up of all the galaxies, stars, planets, moons, asteroids and other bodies scattered through the emptiness of space.

Edwin Mattison McMillan (1907–1991)
McMillan is a United States physicist who in 1940 made the first element heavier than uranium (element 92). He used neutrons accelerated in a particle accelerator to bombard uranium atoms and produced atoms of element 93, which he called neptunium. For this work, he shared the 1951 Nobel Prize in Chemistry.

the Universe is like trying to find the 'end' of a circle.

The visible Universe contains millions of galaxies, collected into clusters and superclusters. These clusters are arranged in a clumpy way instead of being scattered fairly evenly through space. Explaining this 'clumping' is a major task in COSMOLOGY.

Astronomers have detected remote galaxies and QUASARS many thousands of millions of light-years away. Even these distant objects are made of the same ATOMS as the ones familiar to us, and obey the laws of physics. We are now used to the idea of the Universe being similar everywhere, or 'homogeneous', but it was only about 100 years ago that the law of gravity was proved to operate beyond the Solar System.

Uranium

Uranium is a white METAL. It is an ELEMENT which exists in several varieties, or ISOTOPES, all of which are RADIO-ACTIVE. One of the isotopes, uranium-235, can undergo nuclear fission to release large amounts of ENERGY. It is used in atomic weapons and as the fuel in most types of NUCLEAR REACTORS. Uranium-238 is the fuel in another type of power station, a breeder reactor, which turns it into PLUTONIUM. Uranium occurs in ores such as pitchblende, but is difficult to extract and even more difficult to separate into its isotopes. The mining and extraction of uranium, and its use as a nuclear fuel, create large amounts of radioactive waste products which are difficult to get rid of safely because they have to be sealed in special containers and stored.
See also NUCLEAR PHYSICS; NUCLEAR WASTE.

▲ *These hands hold a piece of uranium-235, the isotope that is used as a fuel in nuclear reactors. Uranium is one of the densest metals; this small piece weighs 4.5 kg and is worth over 200,000 dollars. Before holding the uranium the hands have to be protected with special gloves.*

Glenn Theodore Seaborg (1912–)
Seaborg is a United States chemist who specializes in the transuranic elements (the radioactive elements that are heavier than uranium). From 1940, Seaborg and his team produced nine new elements, from plutonium (element 94) to nobelium (element 102). They described the elements' chemical properties. Seaborg shared the 1951 Nobel Prize in Chemistry.

Uranus Facts
Diameter at equator
52,000 km
Diameter at poles
50,200 km
Distance from Sun
3,007,000,000 km
(maximum)
2,737,000,000 km
(minimum)
Year length 84 y
Day length 17 h 24 min
Mass 14.6 Earths
Density 0.22 Earth
Surface temperature
−200°C

◄ *Uranus has a faint ring system and 15 moons, 5 large ones and 10 small. Its diameter is four times that of Earth.*

Uranus

Uranus became the first planet to be discovered with a TELESCOPE when William Herschel, observing from Bath, England, found it in 1781. Because it is far away, little was known about it before Voyager 2 sent back close-up observations in 1986, although a dim ring system was detected in 1977. The spacecraft photographed 13 main rings and other very narrow and faint ones.

Five satellites have been known for many years, the largest being Titania (1600 km across) and the smallest, Miranda, 480 km across. They are all airless, icy-surfaced bodies with craters where flying fragments crashed into them. Another, Ariel, has immense valleys, while Miranda is a patchwork of completely different markings. One suggestion is that an old satellite was shattered in a collision, and the fragments drifted together so that Miranda is partly 'inside-out'! Voyager discovered 10 new satellites, most less than 50 km across.

Uranus itself is surrounded by a thick ATMOSPHERE of hydrogen, helium and methane. But unlike the other 'cloudy' outer planets it has hardly any cloud markings. The most curious thing about Uranus is the tilt of its axis, which is so tipped over that during its 'year' the Sun can shine almost overhead at each pole, and parts of its surface are bathed in continuous day, and then continuous night, for almost 40 of our years.

Sir William Herschel (1738–1822)
Herschel was a German-born British astronomer who in 1781 discovered the planet Uranus using a telescope he had built. He went to Britain as a musician when he was 19, and took up astronomy when he was 36. As well as discovering Uranus, he identified nearly 2000 nebulae and catalogued 800 double stars. He became astronomer to King George III.

**Edward Jenner
(1749–1823)**
Jenner was a British doctor who in 1796 performed the first successful inoculations against disease. He inoculated people with cowpox (a disease of cattle) to protect them against deadly smallpox. The technique was widely adopted and over the next 100 years deaths from smallpox fell dramatically (from 40 per 10,000 people to 1 per 10,000).

▶ *Vaccination gives active immunity to a disease. It uses killed or weakened germs that have been 'grown' in hen's eggs or laboratory animals. Passive immunity results from inoculation with a serum, usually from an animal which has developed immunity to the disease. It can also be given by using a similar, but less dangerous, live germ.*

722

Vaccination

Vaccination causes the body to produce substances called ANTIBODIES, which fight DISEASE. Substances which do not naturally belong in the body are called antigens. These cause the IMMUNE SYSTEM to react by producing antibodies which make the antigens harmless. Antigens are carried on the surface of bacteria and viruses. Some chemical COMPOUNDS also act as antigens.

In vaccination, the antigens which enter the body, through injection or by mouth, are harmless. The vaccine has been treated to weaken the bacteria or virus, and in some cases, dead bacteria or viruses, or even extracts of the antigen substances, will cause the protective antibodies to be produced. Sometimes further vaccinations or boosters are needed to provide continuing protection against infection. To protect against tuberculosis (TB), a similar live but less dangerous bacterium is used to create an infection which causes the body to develop immunity to TB. This is called *inoculation*, and was first used to protect against smallpox, when people were injected with a milder disease called cowpox.

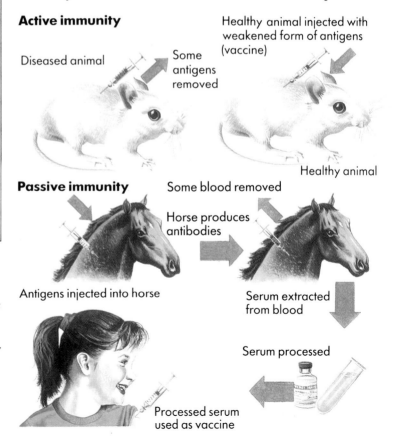

Active immunity

Diseased animal

Some antigens removed

Healthy animal injected with weakened form of antigens (vaccine)

Healthy animal

Passive immunity

Antigens injected into horse

Some blood removed

Horse produces antibodies

Serum extracted from blood

Serum processed

Processed serum used as vaccine

Vacuum

Most of the spaces on Earth which we usually think of as empty are filled with MOLECULES of AIR. A vacuum, on the other hand, is a space which really is empty; a perfect vacuum contains no molecules of any sort. Interstellar space, the open space between the STARS, is very nearly a perfect vacuum. It is difficult to make a vacuum. It is necessary to pump out all the air from inside a container. However, molecules of air can leak in through very tiny

Steam

Metal container

Cap on

Air pressure

Boiling water

holes in the container and molecules on the surface of the container evaporate into the empty space. The container must also be strong enough to withstand the inward PRESSURE of the air outside. Something which is nearly a vacuum is called a *partial vacuum*. A vacuum is useful as thermal INSULATION because it prevents heat flow by CONVECTION. Foods such as coffee which become stale when exposed to air, are packed in a 'vacuum pack' from which the air has been removed.

See also EVAPORATION; MAGDEBURG SPHERES.

Vacuum flask

A vacuum flask is a container used to keep liquids or gases hot or cold. It is also known as a Thermos flask or a Dewar flask after the Scottish scientist, Sir James Dewar, who invented it in the 1890s. It is made from a double-walled glass bottle. The air in the gap between the two glass walls is pumped out to create a VACUUM. The walls facing into the vacuum are silvered like a MIRROR. The vacuum prevents HEAT from passing across the

Many people talk about 'hoovering' the carpet, meaning to clean it using a vacuum cleaner. Hoover was the name of an inventor who made a vacuum cleaner and founded the company that still bears his name. There are other trade names such as Thermos and Biro which have passed into the language.

◄ *Any container with a lower pressure on the inside than on the outside must be very strong. If a little water is boiled in a metal can, the water produces steam which expands. If the can is taken off the heat and the cap screwed on, the steam will cool and condense lowering the pressure inside the can, forming a partial vacuum. After a short time, the air pressure will crush the can inwards.*

▼ *An upright vacuum cleaner has an electric motor that sucks air from the bottom of the dust bag. This leaves a partial vacuum which causes dust to be pushed up by the outside air pressure into the bag.*

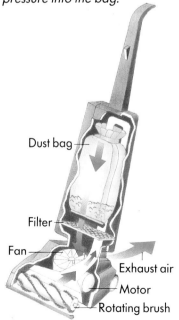

Dust bag

Filter

Fan

Exhaust air

Motor

Rotating brush

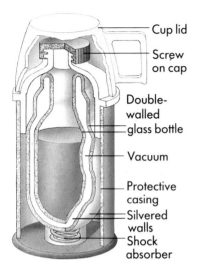

Cup lid

Screw on cap

Double-walled glass bottle

Vacuum

Protective casing

Silvered walls

Shock absorber

Sir James Dewar (1842–1923)
Dewar was a British chemist and physicist who in about 1892 invented the vacuum flask, also called a Dewar flask. It is sometimes known by its trade name, Thermos flask. Dewar used the flask in experiments with liquid oxygen, hydrogen and other gases at very low temperatures. In 1891, with Frederick Abel, he developed cordite, a smokeless propellant explosive for cartridges and shells.

▲ A vacuum flask keeps hot liquids hot or cold liquids cold by preventing the transfer of heat between the contents and the outside. The vacuum prevents heat flow by convection, and silvering on the flask's walls prevents heat flow by radiation.

The United States inventor Thomas Edison produced the first vacuum tube, but he did not realize its importance. Early in the 1880s, Edison sealed an extra electrode into a light bulb. He noticed that a current flowed from the bulb's filament to this electrode if it was positively charged. Edison had made a diode vacuum tube, but he could see no use for his invention.

▶ In a diode valve, electrons travel from the heated cathode (negative electrode) to the anode (positive electrode). A triode has a similar arrangement of electrodes but in addition has a control grid. This is between the cathode and anode, and its voltage is adjusted to control the flow of electrons.

gap by contact with air molecules, called CONVECTION. The silvering reflects heat, preventing it from crossing the gap by RADIATION. In 1925 a vacuum flask enclosed in a case for protection first went on sale to the public for carrying hot or cold drinks.

Vacuum tube

A vacuum tube or valve is a device that works by the action of ELECTRONS travelling through a gas or a VACUUM. Inside the valve's glass body, electrons flow from an electrically-heated electrode (the cathode) through the gas or vacuum to a second electrode (the anode). There may be other electrodes between the cathode and anode which control the flow of electrons.

There are different types of valves. The first, the

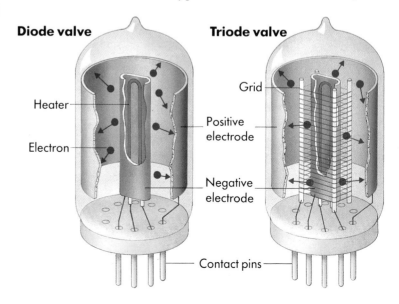

Diode valve

Heater

Electron

Triode valve

Grid

Positive electrode

Negative electrode

Contact pins

724

diode, was invented in 1904. Electrons travel through it in one direction only, enabling it to convert alternating current to direct current. The triode valve, invented in 1910, is used to amplify electrical signals. Other types of valve include the tetrode and pentode. Valves have now been largely replaced by the semiconductor DIODE, TRANSISTOR and INTEGRATED CIRCUIT.

▲ Special vacuum tubes or valves are used to generate radio waves. These large valves were the key components in an early short-wave radio transmitter.

Valency

Valency is the combining power of a chemical ELEMENT. It tells us how many chemical BONDS an element can form when it combines with other elements in COMPOUNDS. These bonds involve ELECTRONS, and so the valency is the number of electrons an element can give, take or share in forming bonds. Some elements always have the same valency. For hydrogen it is always one, for oxygen it is two and for carbon it is four. Other elements have more than one valency. Iron, for example, can combine to form compounds in two ways and so has a valency of two in some of its compounds, and in other compounds its valency is three.

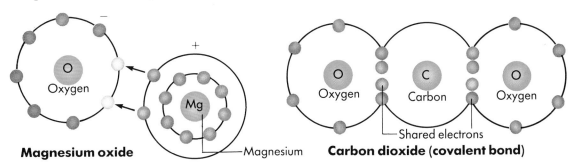

Magnesium oxide — Magnesium   **Carbon dioxide (covalent bond)**

Shared electrons

▲ Magnesium and oxygen both have a valency of two. The left-hand diagram shows how magnesium can give its two outer electrons to fill oxygen's outer shell (to give it eight electrons), forming the compound magnesium oxide. Carbon has four outer electrons and a valency of four. The right-hand diagram shows how one atom of carbon can combine with two oxygen atoms to form carbon dioxide.

Van Allen belts

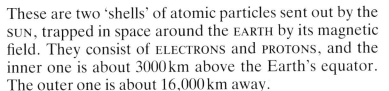

These are two 'shells' of atomic particles sent out by the SUN, trapped in space around the EARTH by its magnetic field. They consist of ELECTRONS and PROTONS, and the inner one is about 3000 km above the Earth's equator. The outer one is about 16,000 km away.

The Van Allen belts are denser places in the Earth's magnetosphere. The magnetosphere is a huge volume of space, pushed into a comet shape by the SOLAR WIND, extending about 100,000 km towards the Sun and a million or so away from it. At the edge of the magnetosphere, the Earth's magnetic field meets that of the Sun.

These two magnetic fields are like a vast GENERATOR

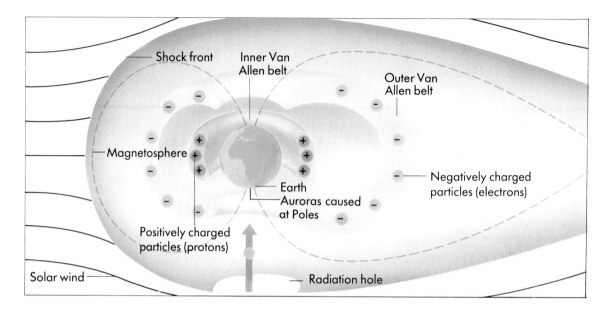

Shock front — Inner Van Allen belt — Outer Van Allen belt — Magnetosphere — Earth — Auroras caused at Poles — Positively charged particles (protons) — Negatively charged particles (electrons) — Solar wind — Radiation hole

▲ *The Van Allen radiation belts around the Earth are part of the magnetosphere. The belts are distorted by the solar wind so that they are much closer to the surface of the Earth on the side of the Earth that faces the Sun.*

creating ELECTRICITY, and the ENERGY is carried down by particles into the Earth's atmosphere, causing the glows known as AURORAS. These two belts were discovered in 1958 by the US physicist James Van Allen.

Van de Graaff generator

A Van de Graaff generator is a machine used to produce very high voltages. It was invented in the 1930s by the US physicist, Robert Jemison Van de Graaff. It consists of a hollow metal hemisphere or dome supported on top of an insulated pillar. A belt made from an electrical INSULATOR is wound around two rollers, one at the top of the pillar inside the dome and one at the bottom. The

Scientists planning the first Apollo trips to the Moon were worried about the effects of the radiation in the Van Allen belts on the astronauts. It turned out that there was less danger than had been feared. The thickness of the spacecraft's skin was enough to protect the astronauts.

▶ *At a science demonstration, a high-voltage charge of static electricity from a Van de Graaff generator makes this girl's hair stand on end. Each hair tries to push away from the next one because the like charges repel and the hairs all have the same static charge.*

belt is driven around the rollers. As the belt travels past a row of metal points next to the bottom roller, it acquires a positive charge. The belt carries the charge up inside the dome where it is transferred to the dome and moves to the dome's outer surface. The charge continues to build up on the dome, which may reach an electric potential of up to 13 million volts (13 MV).
See also STATIC ELECTRICITY.

Vapour

A vapour is a GAS that can exist at the same TEMPERATURE as the LIQUID or SOLID from which it comes. Unlike a gas above a certain temperature, a vapour can be liquefied by PRESSURE alone without being cooled.

After it has been raining and the Sun comes out, any puddles soon dry up. This is because when a liquid such as rainwater evaporates, ATOMS or MOLECULES leave its surface and form a vapour. When a liquid is heated, it changes to a vapour more rapidly than when the surroundings are cold. For example when water boils, it changes to a vapour, in this case STEAM, very quickly. If a vapour is cooled, it changes back into a liquid. In a steamy room, water vapour (steam) condenses on the window to form water. Sometimes when the temperature drops at the end of the day, water vapour in the air condenses as droplets of water that form mist or fog.

If a vapour is compressed, it changes back into a liquid. This cycle of changes is used in REFRIGERATION. A vapour is compressed to make a liquid, and then the

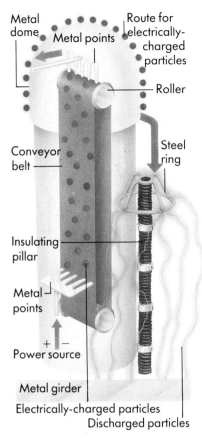

▲ *A Van de Graaff generator uses a conveyor belt to carry electric charge and store it on a metal dome. The charge is picked up from a metal comb connected to a high-voltage electricity supply. A large enough charge of discharged particles (at millions of volts) can jump from the steel ring, ionizing the surrounding air and flashing to the ground like artificial lightning.*

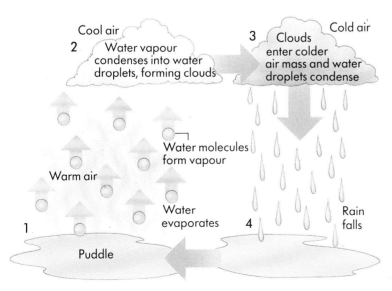

◄ *1 Puddles dry up in the Sun as the water in them is changed to vapour. High in the sky, the vapour forms clouds of water droplets 2. These droplets combine to form drops of rain when the cloud is cooled 3. The rain falls and the water that lies on the ground forms puddles 4.*

liquid is allowed to evaporate back into a vapour. This stage requires HEAT and the heat is taken from the inside of the refrigerator, so keeping the contents cool.
See also CONDENSATION; EVAPORATION.

Variable stars

Most stars shine with a steady light, but some vary in brightness over periods from hours to years. A few of these 'variable' stars do not actually change in light output at all, but appear to do so because they are twin or BINARY STARS. As they orbit each other, the light from one is blocked out for a time, and they are known as eclipsing binaries. True variables are usually unstable single stars that swell out and shrink, or binary stars where gas passes from one to the other and suddenly flares up. The unstable stars usually repeat their

▲ *Clouds of vapour form round a horse's nostrils. In the cold air, water vapour in the animal's breath condenses to form minute droplets of water.*

▶ *Variable stars change in brightness. Sometimes this is not because the star flares up or dims. For example, a binary star consists of two stars orbiting each other. It appears bright when both stars are visible and less bright when one is hidden behind the other.*

▼ *The brightness of a variable star changes as the star swells and shrinks. Many of these stars pulsate regularly at a rate of a few hours or days.*

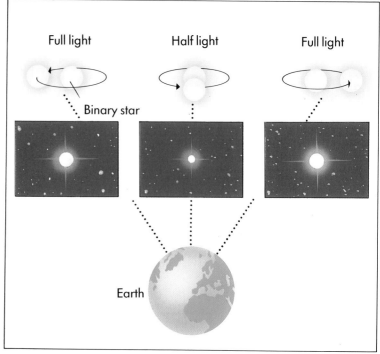

Full light   Half light   Full light

Binary star

Earth

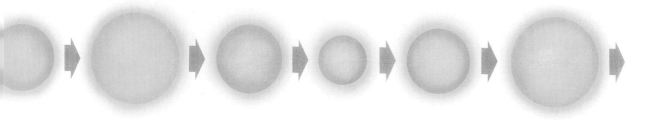

brightenings and fadings at regular intervals, while the explosive binaries are unpredictable. Other types of variables include flare stars (single stars that have brilliant surges of light), and the rare stars that are usually bright, but become dim as clouds form over their surface.

Velocity

Velocity is the rate at which an object's position changes. Velocity involves two pieces of information: the first is the speed at which the object is moving, and the second is the direction in which it is moving. If either of these two things changes, then the velocity changes, so two objects travelling with the same speed in different directions have different velocities. It is important not to confuse speed and velocity: speed refers to how fast an object is moving while velocity refers not only to the object's speed but to the direction it is moving in as well. The rate of change of the velocity is called the ACCELERATION, and the rate of change of position of an object is called speed. Velocity and acceleration are important in MECHANICS, the study of moving things.

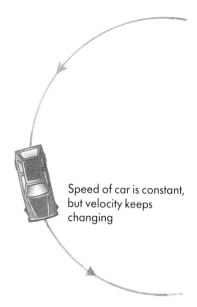

Speed of car is constant, but velocity keeps changing

▲ Speed is the rate of change of position – how far something goes in a given time. Velocity is the speed in a particular direction. So a car driving in a circle can have a constant speed, but its velocity keeps on changing because the car keeps pointing in a different direction.

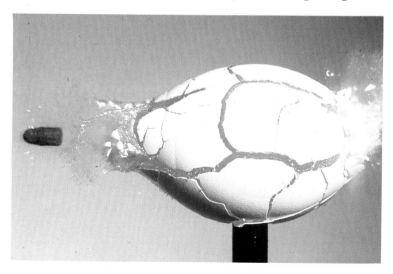

◄ A camera freezes the action as a bullet travelling at a velocity of 450 m/s (nearly one and a half times faster than sound travels) hits a raw egg.

Velocity is measured in units such as metres per second (m/s). One kilometre per hour (1 km/h) is equal to 0.28 m/s. The theory of RELATIVITY tells us that the largest possible velocity is the velocity of light, which is about 300 million metres per second.
See also CENTRIFUGAL FORCE; MOVEMENT AND MOTION.

Stopping Distances
The faster vehicles are travelling, the greater the distance of road they need to stop in. An ordinary car travelling at 50 km/h (31 miles per hour) needs about 23 m to come to a stop, whereas a car travelling at 80 km/h (50 miles per hour) needs 53 m. This is because of the momentum of the vehicle which combines its velocity and its mass. A large lorry needs more room to stop in than a smaller vehicle.

Vein *See* Circulation

Venus Facts
Diameter at equator
12,104 km
Diameter at poles
12,400 km
Distance from Sun
109,000,000 km (maximum)
108,000,000 km (minimum)
Year length 225 d
Day length 117 d
Mass 0.82 Earths
Density 0.89 Earth
Surface temperature
480°C (maximum)

► *The baking hot surface of Venus is hidden behind the dense clouds of its thick, poisonous atmosphere.*

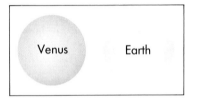

▲ *Venus is about the same size as Earth. Unusually, Venus takes longer to spin on its axis (243 days) than it takes the planet to orbit the Sun (225 days).*

▼ *The space probe Magellan has sent back to Earth the best pictures yet of Venus. The planet is possibly the most unpleasant place in the Solar System.*

Magellan

Venus

Venus is a PLANET that orbits the SUN between the EARTH and MERCURY, and is almost exactly the same size as the Earth. But it is very different from our planet. The surface of Venus is the hottest place in the SOLAR SYSTEM, with a temperature reaching 480°C. It is a rocky windswept planet with an 'atmosphere' that would feel thicker than ocean water at a depth of several hundred metres. This atmosphere contains carbon dioxide, sulphuric acid and other poisonous compounds, and lightning flickers between the clouds.

Sunlight falls on the rocky surface that warms up and gives out heat RADIATION. The carbon dioxide surrounding Venus lets in enough sunlight to heat the ground, but does not let out the heat radiated from the ground. The heat is trapped, releasing more carbon dioxide from the rocks and making the heat blanket even more efficient. This 'runaway GREENHOUSE EFFECT' has turned Venus into an oven.

The invisible surface has been mapped by RADAR from Earth and from SPACE PROBES. Mountain peaks up to 12 km high have been charted. Some features look like Earth-type VOLCANOES. From measurements of the sulphur dioxide gas in Venus' atmosphere, it appears that one or more of the volcanoes may still be active, throwing out sulphur dioxide when it erupts.

Very high frequency (VHF)

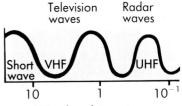

Very high frequency (VHF) is the name given to RADIO waves whose FREQUENCY is higher than the frequency of other radio waves but not as high as ULTRA HIGH FREQUENCY waves (UHF). VHF waves have frequencies of around 100 MHz (one hundred million cycles per second), while other radio waves have frequencies of up to only a few hundred kHz (a few hundred thousand hertz). The higher frequency of VHF means that the signal can carry much more information than ordinary radio waves. The disadvantage of VHF signals,

▲ *VHF radio waves, which lie between short waves and radar waves in the electromagnetic spectrum, are mainly used for television and high-quality radio broadcasting.*

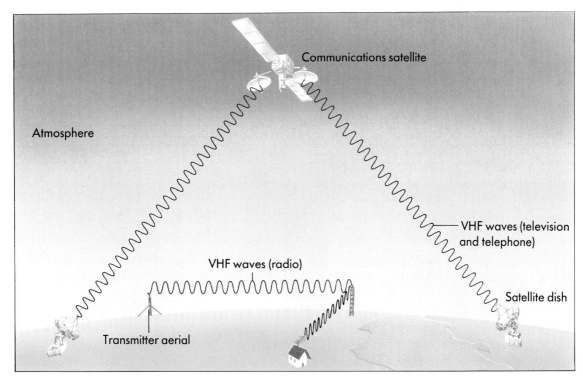

however, is that they are not diffracted very easily over hills and, unlike lower-frequency radio waves, they are not reflected from the IONOSPHERE. This means that they are not so effective in transmitting radio signals over very long distances or in mountainous areas.

VHF radio signals are usually different from others because the frequency, rather than the amplitude, of the radio wave is changed when the sound signal is added to the carrier wave. This is called frequency modulation (FM) rather than amplitude modulation (AM).

▲ *VHF radio waves travel in straight lines and so can be used for communication only between places that are within sight of each other. Even with a very tall mast for the transmitting aerial this gives an effective range of only about 80 km overland. But communications satellites allow much greater ranges, and VHF signals to and from a satellite can span an ocean or a whole continent.*

Vesalius, Andreas *See* Muscles

VETERINARY MEDICINE

Veterinary medicine is concerned with the health and treatment of animals. Experiments and surgery on animals have been used for centuries to train doctors, but now veterinary medicine is a highly specialized science in its own right. The training is similar to that for doctors, but is in some ways more complicated, because of the many different animals which must be studied. The veterinary surgeon must be highly skilled at making a diagnosis because, unlike humans, animals cannot help by describing how they feel.

Veterinary medicine can be divided into two groups. Small animal veterinary medicine is concerned with the health and treatment of domestic animals such as cats, dogs and other small pets. A large animal veterinary practice looks after farm livestock and horses, and is generally concerned with preventing illness in these animals, as much as treating them once they are sick. Veterinary surgeons routinely treat farm livestock to remove worms and other parasites which slow their growth or reduce milk production. Vaccines are available to prevent many diseases of domestic pets and farm livestock, by immunizing them against common diseases.

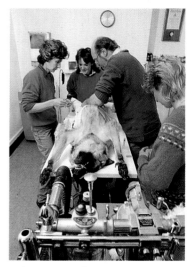

▲ In towns and cities, veterinary surgeons see mainly domestic animals kept as pets by people in the town or city. They treat these animals when ill or injured but also, just as children can be immunized against common diseases, many pets are vaccinated and receive other preventative care. Here a dog is undergoing surgery.

◄ In agricultural communities, veterinary surgeons treat farm animals to keep them healthy and prevent the outbreak of diseases. Herds of cattle or other groups of animals are at danger from epidemics of animal diseases because the disease can spread very quickly. Whole herds of animals could die and infect the animals belonging to other farmers nearby. On this farm, the cattle are being given an injection of a drug to combat internal parasites.

Some Common Animal Diseases

Animal diseases need to be treated before the disease can spread to other animals. Many animal diseases can be transmitted to humans.
Brucellosis an infectious disease of cattle, goats and pigs which causes fever.
Psittacosis a viral disease of parrots and other birds that is similar to pneumonia.
Rabies a very infectious viral disease which affects the nervous system and in dogs, causes foaming at the mouth.
Tuberculosis an infectious disease which mostly affects the lungs. Tuberculosis in cattle can be passed to humans.

Veterinary surgeons treat some exotic animals such as gorillas, lions and tigers. All of these need dental care in captivity. Special techniques are used to help breed some endangered species. Veterinary surgeons are employed by zoos and safari parks to keep rare animals healthy.

See also AGRICULTURE; BIOLOGY; BREEDING; DISEASE; ENDANGERED SPECIES; PARASITE; PATHOLOGY; VACCINATION; ZOOLOGY.

Video camera

A video camera is used to convert an image into an electrical signal that can form a picture on a TELEVISION screen or be recorded on video TAPE.

Light enters the camera through a LENS. This bends the light rays together so that they form a sharp image on a light-sensitive plate called a target. The target is normally charged up to about 30 volts. When light falls on it, the voltage leaks away. A brightly lit part of the target may fall to zero volts. The pick-up tube produces an ELECTRON beam that scans across the target. It restores each part of the target to its fully charged state. The bright parts of the target require greater charging than the darker parts. This charging current forms the video signal from the camera.

Although many cameras used in television studios still have pick-up tubes, most home video cameras and camcorders (a camcorder is a combined camera and recorder) use a different light sensor called a charge coupled device or CCD. This SEMICONDUCTOR device is much smaller than a pick-up tube, is less fragile than the glass tube and it is not damaged by exposure to very bright light as the pick-up tube can be.
See also VIDEO RECORDER.

All cameras have to be held steady so that the pictures produced will be clear. Originally, movie cameras used to have to run on rails similar to those used by trains to keep them steady. Steadicam is a system that allows a video camera operator to move around freely without the picture becoming wobbly and unsteady. It has a harness for the camera operator and a system of springs and levers to absorb any sudden movements. It works something like the way the suspension of a car does.

Camcorder

▶ *A modern amateur video camera, called a camcorder, records pictures and sound on a small cassette of video tape. The tape can be played back through an ordinary television using a video recorder.*

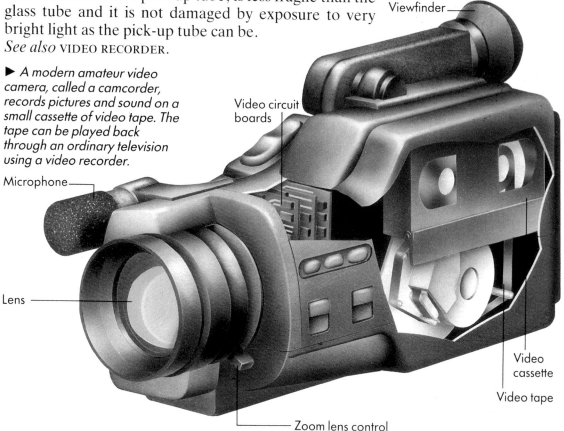

Viewfinder

Video circuit boards

Microphone

Lens

Zoom lens control

Video cassette

Video tape

Video recorder

A video recorder is a machine used to store moving pictures on magnetic TAPE. It receives signals through a cable connected to the TELEVISION aerial. As in a CASSETTE RECORDER, the tape is held against a spinning metal drum containing the recording heads. The drum is set at an angle to the tape. Each revolution of the drum records a single television picture across the width of the tape. To record, an erase head removes any existing magnetic pattern from the tape and a video head records new picture signals as a diagonal pattern on the magnetic tape. Sound signals are recorded along one edge of the tape by the audio head.

The first video recorder was developed in 1956 by the US Ampex Corporation. It recorded television pictures a line at a time across the width of 50mm-wide magnetic tape. The first video recorder for home use was developed by the European Philips company in 1972. The most popular home video system or format is now VHS, the Video Home System developed by JVC in Japan in the mid 1970s. It uses cassettes of 12.65mm-wide tape.

▲ *Modern home video recorders often have a wide variety of features to control both recording and playback. Many now have remote control devices that send infrared signals to the recorder to operate these features.*

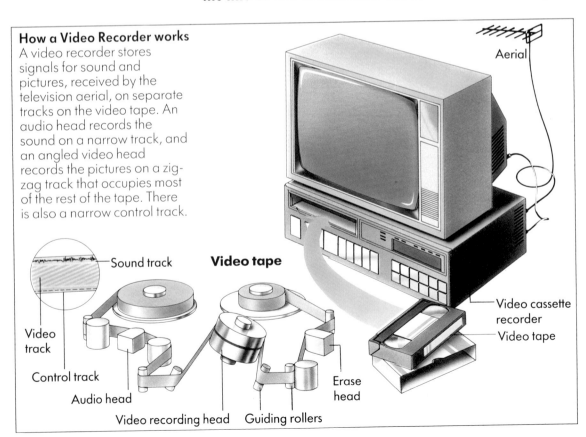

How a Video Recorder works
A video recorder stores signals for sound and pictures, received by the television aerial, on separate tracks on the video tape. An audio head records the sound on a narrow track, and an angled video head records the pictures on a zig-zag track that occupies most of the rest of the tape. There is also a narrow control track.

Aerial

Sound track

Video tape

Video track

Control track

Audio head

Video recording head

Guiding rollers

Erase head

Video cassette recorder

Video tape

VIRUSES AND VIRAL DISEASES 🔲

Viruses are tiny organisms which nearly always produce diseases in animals and plants. All viruses are parasites which can live only in other life forms. Technically, they are not living creatures at all, because they can reproduce and carry out the normal processes of life only when they are inside a cell, and forming a part of the cell's structure. Viruses invade cells and take over the genetic material (DNA and RNA), changing its function so that the whole cell becomes a 'factory' producing viruses. Eventually the cell bursts and dies, releasing the new viruses to spread.

Because the function of the cell is affected, infection with viruses nearly always causes disease. The body's usual defences cannot easily fight the virus, because once the virus is inside the cell, the body's immune system is unable to recognize the invader. Antibodies can attack the virus only when it bursts out of the cell ready to infect other cells. Drugs such as antibiotics do not work against viruses, and the immune system must be relied upon to fight the infection. The HIV virus, which can cause AIDS, is particularly dangerous because it infects and kills the cells of the immune system which normally fight diseases. Virus particles, or virions, are very tiny. Viral diseases are usually spread by viruses carried in water droplets in the air, which are inhaled into the lungs. Colds and influenza are common infections caused by viruses.

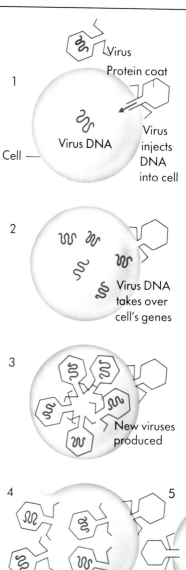

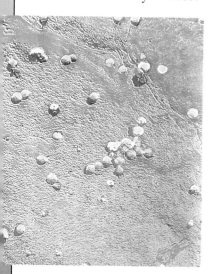

▲ A false-colour picture taken with an electron microscope shows particles of the virus adenovirus (yellow), similar to the type that cause the common cold. The tiny organism is magnified here 25,000 times.

Viral Diseases

Diseases caused by viruses include some of the most dangerous and most annoying of all illnesses. Some of them (but by no means all) can be prevented by vaccination, but treatment is usually limited to relieving the symptoms. Antibiotics, effective against most bacterial diseases, are useless against viruses. Viral diseases include:
AIDS (acquired immune deficiency syndrome)
Chickenpox
Common cold
Influenza
Measles
Mumps
Polio
Rabies
Rubella (German measles)

▲ A virus consists of a strand of genetic material (DNA or RNA) inside a protein coat. It infects a cell by injecting its DNA into the cell **1**. The viral DNA takes over the cell **2** and makes the cell produce more viruses **3**. Eventually the infected cell bursts **4**, releasing the new viruses that go on to attack more cells **5**.

See also AIDS; ANTIBIOTICS; ANTIBODIES AND ANTIGENS; CELL; DISEASE; IMMUNE SYSTEM; INFECTION; PARASITE; VACCINATION.

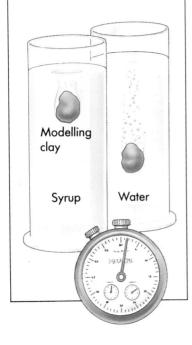

Modelling clay

Syrup   Water

Viscosity

Viscosity describes the ability of FLUIDS (GASES or LIQUIDS) to flow. The property of flowing is called the fluidity, resistance to flow is the viscosity. It is a type of FRICTION force. If an object is moved through a fluid, the fluid just next to the object is carried along with it. The nearby fluid is therefore moving relative to the fluid further away from the object and the resistance which is produced pulls the object back. This backwards force from the viscosity can be reduced by STREAMLINING. Different fluids have different viscosities; a gas such as air has a very low viscosity, since the MOLECULES in it do not pull on each other very much. A liquid such as cooking oil has a high viscosity because its molecules have long 'tails' on them which easily get tangled up and stop the molecules moving past each other.

Visual display unit (VDU)

A visual display unit or VDU is part of a COMPUTER. It shows visual information such as text and COMPUTER GRAPHICS on a screen. The most common type of VDU is the CATHODE RAY TUBE or CRT. A CRT works like a TELEVISION screen. It builds up the picture from hundreds of lines of glowing phosphor dots. It may be monochrome (single-colour) or colour. Alternatives to the CRT include the plasma panel, LIQUID CRYSTAL DISPLAY (LCD) and electroluminescent display. They use glowing NEON gas, LIQUID CRYSTALS and glowing phosphors respectively to form images. These flat panel displays are more compact and less fragile than the glass CRT.

▶ A visual display unit, or VDU, connected to a computer can show alphanumeric characters (letters and numbers) so can be used with word-processing software to display text. VDUs can also be used with computer graphics programs to display graphs and charts.

Vitamins

Vitamins are substances that our bodies need to help the many CHEMICAL REACTIONS which take place inside the CELLS. They often act as CATALYSTS. Vitamins cannot be made inside the body (except some vitamin D can be made in the skin), so they must be obtained from the food we eat. There are several types of vitamins, which are found in a very wide range of foods. Some vitamins dissolve in body fat and can be stored in this way, so they are needed only in very small amounts in our food. Others such as vitamin C dissolve in water, and are flushed out in our urine, so we need to top up the amounts in our body constantly. Vitamins, and MINERALS, are important nutrients which help to build cells.

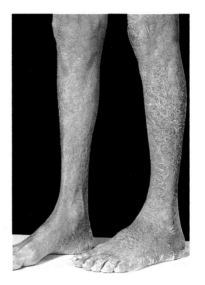

▲ This person is suffering from pellagra. This disorder results from a lack of one type of vitamin B in the diet and causes broken skin and weakness in the muscles. The type of vitamin B missing is needed by the body to obtain energy from glucose. Without it the tissues of the body lose a lot of energy.

Vitamin	Usual Sources	Action in Body
Vitamin A	Liver, fish oils, dairy products, fruit and vegetables	Needed for healthy eyes, skin and tissues
Vitamin B (several types)	Meat, dairy products, whole grains (as in wholemeal flour and bread), vegetables	Used by cells in the release of energy, and in red blood cell production
Vitamin C (ascorbic acid)	Oranges, lemons, many other fruits, and vegetables	Needed for healthy bones and teeth, and for tissue repair
Vitamin D	Oily fish, dairy products and eggs. Some vitamin D is made in the skin by sunlight.	Needed for bone growth
Vitamin E	Brown flour, wheat-germ, liver, green vegetables	In humans no proved function
Vitamin K	Leafy vegetables. Also made in the intestines by harmless bacteria	Helps with blood clotting

In Western countries, the type and amounts of food available mean that people are very rarely deficient in vitamins or minerals. Where famine and malnutrition are common, vitamin deficiency can be serious, particularly in children. Deficiencies of vitamin D cause rickets, in which the bones do not harden properly, so the legs become curved and deformed. This often affects children eating mostly rice, even though some vitamin D can be made when sunlight falls on the skin. Vitamin supplements are not necessary if a balanced diet is eaten.

▲ A properly balanced diet will contain all the vitamins that a person needs. It should include milk and dairy products, bread, meat and fish or pulses, and plenty of fresh fruit and vegetables.

▶ *An erupting volcano can produce thousands of tonnes of lava. Red-hot lava can have a temperature of over 1000°C.*

The world's most devastating volcanic eruption took place at Tambora, Indonesia in 1815 when 12,000 people were killed. The volcano threw out about 150 cubic km of ash and dust, and lost 1250 m in height. Later in the 19th century when Krakatau, also in Indonesia, exploded, 35,000 people were drowned by a giant wave (tsunami).

Volcano Facts
There are about 850 active volcanoes in the world of which 75 percent are part of the 'Ring of Fire'. The word 'volcano' comes from the Latin name *Volcanus* for the ancient god of fire. Near Sicily, Italy, there is an island called Vulcano with an active volcano on it.

The best-documented volcanic eruption was that of Mount St Helens in the north western United States in 1980. For several weeks before the eruption the volcano's activity was monitored by scientists. Despite all this care 60 people died, one of whom was one of the observing scientists. He was too close because the eruption was more powerful than expected.

▶ *Most volcanoes are found along or close to the edges of the plates that make up the Earth's crust. The plates float on the Earth's red-hot core. Their movements cause the flow of hot material to the surface that leads to volcanic eruptions.*

Volcanoes

Volcanoes are the various vents or cracks in the crust of the EARTH through which molten rock or LAVA, gas, steam, ash and even solid ROCK material may be forced out to the surface. The shape of a volcano depends largely on the type of material forced out.

Volcanic eruptions take place in those parts of the Earth's crust where there is a large flow of heat from within the mantle. This is usually along the margins of plates that carry the land and sea. Some volcanoes, such as those which make up the Hawaiian islands, occur within a plate itself and these tend to be less violent than

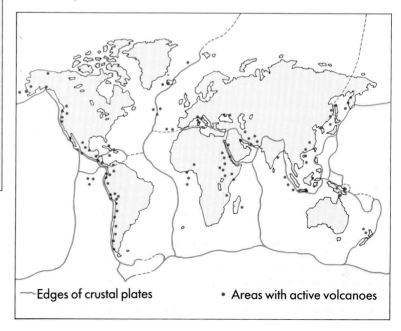

⌒ Edges of crustal plates   • Areas with active volcanoes

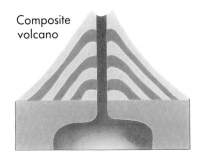
Composite volcano

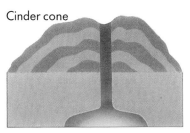
Cinder cone

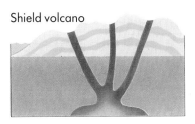
Shield volcano

▲ *There are three main types of volcano which each have distinctive cones. A composite volcano erupts regularly, spilling* | *out lava and cinders that flow down the sides and cool to form a cone-shaped mountain. A cinder volcano throws out ash* | *and builds a flatter cone. A shield volcano is flatter still and has several openings where lava wells up to the surface.*

those which occur at plate margins. There are so many volcanoes around the boundary of the Pacific plate that it is known as the 'Pacific ring of fire'.

Volcanoes, such as those of the Hawaiian islands, force out large amounts of thin lava so that the volcanic cone is low and spreads out to cover a wide area. Layer after layer of lava, ash and debris builds up gradually to form the elegantly shaped cone.

In some volcanoes, the vent becomes blocked between eruptions by a plug of rock. Slowly, the pressure under the plug builds up and the volcano erupts with such force and speed that no one has any time to escape. For example, the ancient city of Pompeii in south-west Italy was buried by an eruption of Vesuvius in AD 79.

Volt

The volt is the SI UNIT that measures voltage. Voltage is also known as electromotive force (e.m.f.) or 'potential difference'. This is the difference in the ENERGY of an electric charge at two different points. One volt is the potential difference between two points if one JOULE of energy is needed to take one COULOMB of charge between the points. One volt of potential difference across a RESISTANCE of one ohm produces a current of one AMPERE. Electric charges flow, if they can, to the point where their energy is lowest so the potential difference, or voltage, is the driving force for currents.

Voltages are measured using a voltmeter; these can work by using the voltage to be measured to send an electric current through a resistance. The magnetic field of this current then moves the needle on the voltmeter's scale to show how many volts are flowing. More accurate

SEE FOR YOURSELF
The molten rock called magma moves through the Earth's crust under pressure. You can produce a similar effect if you roll up a nearly-finished tube of toothpaste. The pressure squeezes the paste towards the cap. Make a small hole near the cap and keep squeezing, toothpaste will ooze out of the hole like lava from a volcano.

► *The voltage between two points in a circuit is measured using a voltmeter. The voltmeter has a high internal resistance. It works by using the magnetic effect of the small current flowing through it to produce movement which makes a needle move round a scale. The size of the current affects the amount the needle moves against the scale and this indicates the size of voltage.*

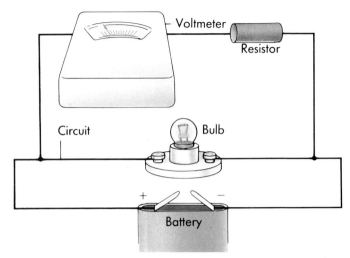

The discovery of vulcanization in 1838 was a turning point in the rubber industry. Before then, rubber products were of little use because they stiffened in winter and became soft and sticky in summer. Then, one day, Charles Goodyear accidentally dropped a rubber sulphur mixture he was experimenting with onto a hot stove. Instead of melting, the rubber became firm.

DIGITAL voltmeters are often used today. The volt is named after the Italian scientist Alessandro Volta.
See also ELECTRICITY; GALVANOMETER.

Volta, Alessandro *See* Electricity

Volume *See* Measurement

Vulcanizing

Vulcanizing is a process for hardening rubber. The RUBBER extracted from the tree is sticky and plastic. It is vulcanized by heating with SULPHUR or sulphur compounds. The MOLECULES in unvulcanized rubber have a long zigzag shape. They straighten when the rubber is stretched and break fairly easily. Vulcanizing causes the long molecules to form chemical BONDS that join them side to side. This makes the rubber tougher and stronger. It still stretches when pulled, but snaps back to its former shape when the force is removed.
See also ELASTICITY.

▼ *Unvulcanized rubber is soft and easily broken, as used in a rubber, or eraser, for rubbing out pencil marks. Heating rubber with sulphur causes chemical bonds to form between the rubber's long hydrocarbon molecules. The resulting vulcanized rubber is very much harder and stronger, and is used for making vehicle tyres and other hard articles.*

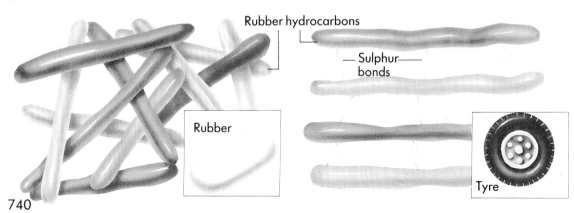

Wankel engine

The Wankel engine is a type of INTERNAL COMBUSTION ENGINE. It was invented by the German engineer, Felix Wankel, in the 1950s. In an ordinary engine, the up and down motion of the pistons has to be converted into a rotary motion to drive the wheels. The link between the engine and wheels could be simplified if the pistons themselves rotated. In the Wankel engine, a triangular piston rotates inside a chamber shaped like an eight. As it rotates, FUEL and air are sucked in through a valve, compressed and ignited by an electrical spark. The burning gases expand rapidly and drive the piston round.

The first car powered by a Wankel engine was the NSU Wankel Spyder. Despite the small size of the engine (500cc), the car had a top speed of 152 km/h. The early engines suffered from several problems. The seals between the rotating piston and the chamber wore down, allowing gases to leak from one side of the piston to the others. It used fuel more quickly than other engines and produced high levels of exhaust POLLUTION.

▼ As in most internal combustion engines, the Wankel engine works using a cycle of four stages: drawing in fuel and air (intake), compressing the fuel/air mixture (compression), igniting the mixture to generate power (power) and getting rid of the burnt gases (exhaust). It does this with a single rotating piston and two spark plugs.

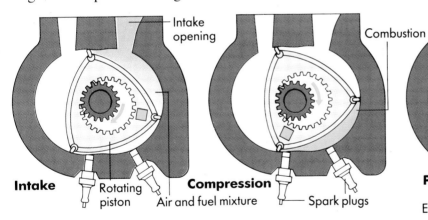

Intake — Intake opening — Rotating piston

Compression — Combustion — Air and fuel mixture — Spark plugs

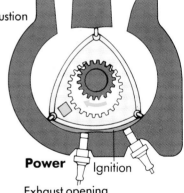

Power — Ignition — Exhaust opening

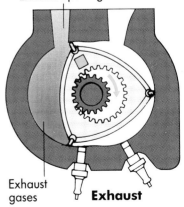

Exhaust gases — Exhaust

Waste disposal

Waste disposal refers to the methods people use to get rid of materials, often called rubbish, which they no longer need. Humans have become a problem for the ENVIRONMENT because of their rapidly increasing population. Human waste or sewage, for example, needs treatment to make it harmless. Sewage is sometimes disposed of into the sea. This can lead to overloading of the natural processes of decay which can spread disease or cause rapid growths of possibly harmful algae.

People produce huge quantities of waste. Containers,

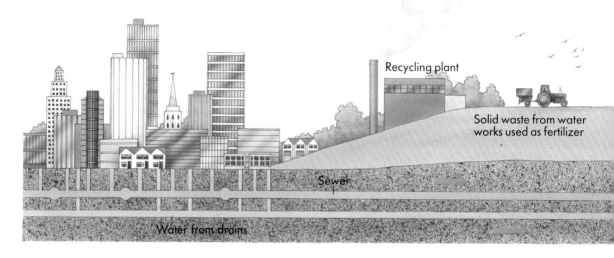

Recycling plant

Solid waste from water works used as fertilizer

Sewer

Water from drains

▲ *Most wastes have to be treated to make them safe before they are released into the environment. An exception is rainwater that runs off the surface of the land, and can be piped into a river. Water waste from our homes has to be treated at a sewage works before it can be released.*

such as bottles and cans, which once filled dustbins, can now be recycled via bottle and can banks in many areas. Much of our waste is buried and the sites then used for construction. Other waste is burned in incinerators, usually in large cities. The by-products of many industries can be very poisonous and, in recent years, strict controls have been introduced to prevent companies releasing waste into rivers, the sea, or the atmosphere without treating it first. The NUCLEAR WASTE from nuclear power stations produces separate problems.

▲ *At a well-managed landfill site, waste is compacted together and then sealed off by being covered with soil. It is important that the waste is covered to prevent smells and to stop animals such as rats living in it.*

Water

More than two-thirds of the human body is made of water, and some animals, such as jellyfish, are almost 100 percent water. The very first forms of life which appeared on EARTH evolved in a watery ENVIRONMENT and this transparent LIQUID is vital to every living thing on our planet. *See* pages 744 and 745.

Water pollution

Water in rivers, lakes and streams almost always contains dissolved chemicals or carries debris suspended in it. Water is described as polluted if the amounts or kinds of substances contained in it are likely to cause harm to humans, other animals, plants or the ENVIRONMENT.

Rivers and the sea have traditionally been used for WASTE DISPOSAL. Fast-flowing rivers are able to transport sewage and other waste away to the oceans where the natural processes of decay can usually cope. But, in slower-flowing waters or where more waste is put into

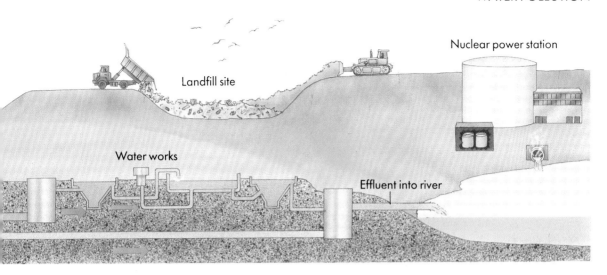

Nuclear power station

Landfill site

Water works

Effluent into river

▲ Although many materials, such as paper, glass and metals, can be separated from wastes and recycled, a lot of waste is still disposed of in landfill sites. Waste from nuclear power stations is reprocessed and stored in sealed containers.

◄ One of the major sources of water pollution is chemical waste from factories being discharged into a river or lake.

the water than can decay naturally, it may be polluted with disease-carrying sewage or with products which may be poisonous to the animals and plants living in it.

Sometimes, water can be polluted by becoming too rich in nourishment, possibly from FERTILIZERS draining from agricultural land. If this happens, certain plants grow rapidly and use up all the oxygen in the water.

In many countries, nowadays, waste products must be treated before they are released into rivers, lakes and seas to prevent water pollution.

▼ Sewage, animal waste and fertilizers can eventually kill off life in a river. Bacteria in the water use oxygen to break-down this organic waste into nutrients. The nutrients encourage the rapid growth of algae. As these die, they add to the organic waste present in the river. The bacteria use so much oxygen to break down all the organic waste that fish cannot breathe and so die.

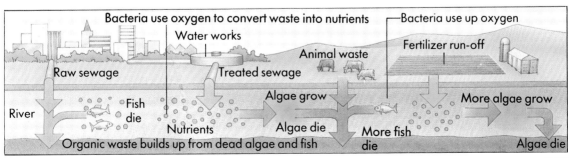

Bacteria use oxygen to convert waste into nutrients

Water works

Bacteria use up oxygen

Fertilizer run-off

Animal waste

Raw sewage

Treated sewage

Algae grow

More algae grow

River

Fish die

Nutrients

Algae die

More fish die

Algae die

Organic waste builds up from dead algae and fish

WATER

Chemically, water is a molecule consisting of two atoms of the gas hydrogen linked by chemical bonds to one atom of the gas oxygen. Pure water, at normal temperatures and pressures, is a tasteless and colourless liquid which lacks any kind of smell. The water we drink, which comes from the water supply, does have a taste because it contains minerals which have dissolved in it when it passed through rocks as groundwater. Water is a very good solvent and is able to dissolve more solids than many other liquids. Water is also good for cleaning because it dissolves dirt. Heating it and adding soap or detergent increases its efficiency. Water is the main component of blood and many substances are carried around the body in this watery liquid. Water also helps to remove some body wastes in the form of another liquid, urine. Water helps animals to keep cool because when animals sweat or pant, the water evaporates, and removes some of their body heat.

Temperature changes the state of water. At temperatures above 100°C it becomes water vapour or the gas, steam. At 0°C water freezes to form solid ice. Most solids become denser than their liquid form when they freeze but water is at its most dense at 4°C when it is still in a liquid form.

Flowing water can be used to turn water wheels to provide power and in hydroelectric schemes is used to provide electricity. It circulates between the atmosphere and the Earth in a process known as the water, or hydrological, cycle.

▲ Water probably has the best known chemical formula: H_2O, that is one oxygen atom and two of hydrogen. It is a remarkable substance, needed for all forms of life.

Sweat   Breathing

Food and drink

70% water

Urine

▲ A person can go without food for several weeks if necessary, but without water life cannot last more than a few days. The human body is 70 percent water. We take it in with food and drink, and lose it in urine, in sweat and in our breath (as water vapour).

▲ Deserts have no free water in streams or lakes, and rain is very rare. There are occasional wells and wet places even in deserts and these are called oases. An oasis is therefore a welcome source of life-giving water to people and animals in these dry environments.
Depending on the amount of water, an oasis may support a few families and their animals or it may eventually support a big city.

◀ Over thousands of years, flowing water can find its way through even the hardest rocks, carving out deep canyons and gorges with its constant pressure. Here the Yellowstone River flows out of the lower (downstream) end of the Grand Canyon in the United States.

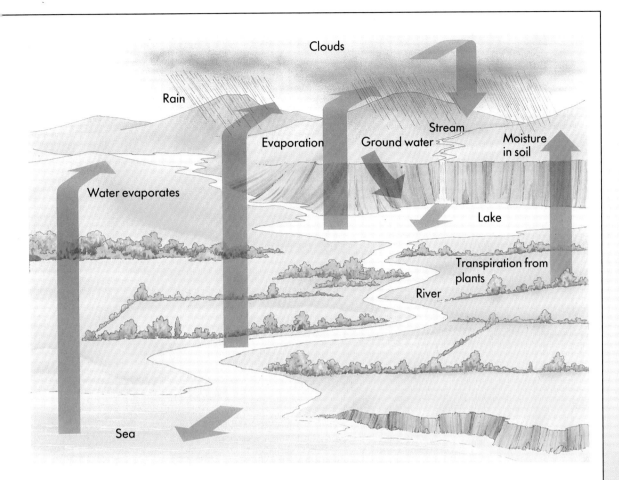

Clouds

Rain

Stream

Evaporation   Ground water

Moisture
in soil

Water evaporates

Lake

Transpiration from
plants

River

Sea

▲ All the water in the world goes round and round in a great cycle. Water that falls as rain soaks into the ground and is taken up by plants or runs off and forms rivers, which flow to the sea. Plants give off water vapour from their leaves, and water in rivers and the sea also evaporates as vapour. The vapour condenses in the atmosphere to form clouds, which produce rain to keep the cycle going.

Water is unusual in that most liquids contract as they cool and freeze, but water contracts to 4°C and then expands as it freezes. This is important for animals because if a pond or river freezes over, the less dense ice floats leaving liquid water beneath in which fish and other animals can survive.

SEE FOR YOURSELF
Water pressure depends on the 'head' of water – the height of the top of the water supply above the level at which it is used. This is because of the pressure exerted by the volume of water above the outlet. You can show this by making a series of holes down the side of a plastic bottle. Cover the holes with sticky tape and fill the bottle with water. Remember to place a bowl on the floor to catch the water before quickly removing the bits of tape. The jet of water where the pressure is greatest (at the bottom of the bottle) squirts out farther than water from near the top.

See also CLOUD; EVAPORATION; GROUNDWATER; HEAVY WATER; HYDRO-ELECTRICITY; HYDROGEN BONDS; ICE; PRECIPITATION; SOLVENT; STEAM.

▲ *In times of drought or in parts of the world where water is in short supply, it may not be possible to pipe water to people's homes. These people have to carry all the water they use from a communal pipe.*

Water supply

A supply of unpolluted fresh WATER is vital for humans. Various methods are used to supply and purify water. Water may be piped from rivers which are reasonably free of POLLUTION. Such water must be filtered and treated to ensure that it is clean. For small-scale supplies, water may be obtained by drilling a well in the ground to below the level of the WATER TABLE. Sometimes GROUNDWATER may be under pressure because of the rock structure. If a well is dug into the water-bearing rocks, the water is forced to the surface under its own pressure as an ARTESIAN WELL. In areas where the population is large, hollows or river valleys may be dammed and flooded to provide reservoirs. In dry parts of the world, water may be piped, or carried in channels, over long distances to irrigate growing crops.

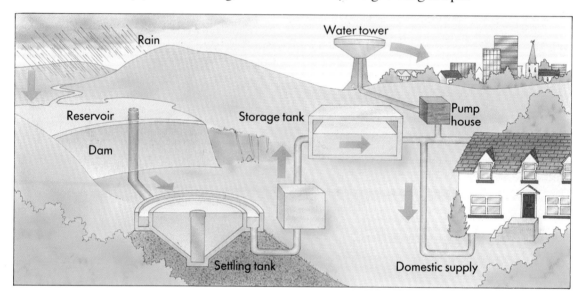

▲ *Water for use in homes and factories is stored in a reservoir, often behind a dam, before being piped to a water works. At the water works, any particles in the water are allowed to settle out in settling tanks and then the water is filtered and treated with chlorine to kill any germs. In some places the purified water is supplied from tall water towers. When water needs to be moved uphill it has to be pumped to overcome gravity.*

Water table

The water table is the top surface of those porous ROCKS which are saturated with GROUNDWATER. In general, the line of the water table follows that of the land surface but it rises and falls depending on the amount of PRECIPITATION that filters into the rocks and on how much WATER is drawn from them. Rock which is saturated with water is referred to as an *aquifer*. The aquifer is not a kind of underground pool. The water is held in the pores and cracks in the rocks.

The SOIL and rocks can be divided into three zones:

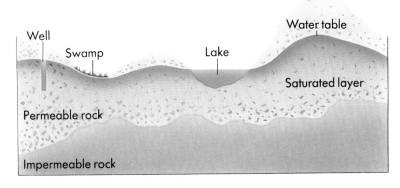

Well Swamp Lake Water table Saturated layer Permeable rock Impermeable rock

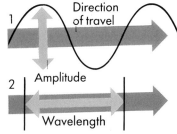

◄ *Water soaks into the ground until it reaches rock that is impermeable to water. The permeable rock above this becomes 'filled' with water up to the level known as the water table. If this level is at the surface, the ground will be wet or swampy. A lake will tend to soak the ground beneath it and raise the water table. A well must be dug deep below the water table to stop it drying out in a drought.*

the zone from the surface down through which water passes to reach the aquifer; the zone which is sometimes saturated; the zone which is permanently saturated, and may be 1000 m deep. A well that will not run dry in a drought must be drilled into this last zone.

Watson, James *See* DNA

Watt

The watt (W) is the SI UNIT of POWER. One watt corresponds to the conversion of one JOULE of ENERGY from one form into another every second. For example, a light bulb uses about 100 watts of power, so it turns 100 joules of electrical energy into heat and light every second, while a one-bar electric fire has a power of about 1000 watts or 1 kilowatt (kW), so it converts 1000 joules of electrical energy into heat every second. The ENGINE of a medium-sized car produces about 50,000 watts (50 kW), while a large electrical power station produces several hundred million watts.
See also KILOWATT-HOUR.

Watt, James *See* Power

Wave

A wave is a disturbance or displacement that repeats itself. Both ELECTROMAGNETIC RADIATION, which includes LIGHT and RADIO waves, and SOUND travel as waves. The simplest kind of wave is called a sine wave. A sine wave is described by its amplitude (the height of the wave) and its WAVELENGTH. In many WAVE MOTIONS, a sine wave travels along without changing its shape at a particular VELOCITY. The number of peaks or troughs of the wave

Powerful Electricity
An electric heater converts electrical energy into heat energy. The rate at which it does this is its power. For example, if it converts 1000 joules of electricity into heat in 1 second, its power is 1000 joules per second or 1000 watts (equal to 1 kilowatt).

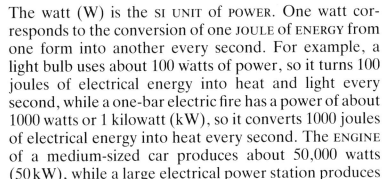

1 Direction of travel Amplitude 2 Wavelength

▲ *The two main properties of a wave are its amplitude and wavelength. The amplitude is the maximum displacement — the height from the crest of a wave to a trough. The wavelength is the distance between two consecutive waves. The number of waves that pass a particular point in a given time gives the frequency of the waves.*

▶ *Refraction, reflection and diffraction are all important properties of waves. Waves are refracted, or bent, when they pass from one substance into another of different density. For example, when sound waves travel from air into a brick wall, they are refracted. They are refracted back to the same original direction when they pass out of the brick and into the air again. Reflection and diffraction are other ways in which waves can be bent. In reflection, the waves bounce off a barrier, just as a light beam bounces off a mirror. Sound echoes are produced when sound waves bounce back off a wall or cliff. In diffraction, the waves spread out after they have passed through a narrow gap in a barrier.*

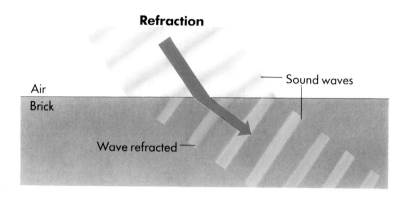

Refraction

Air
Brick

Sound waves

Wave refracted

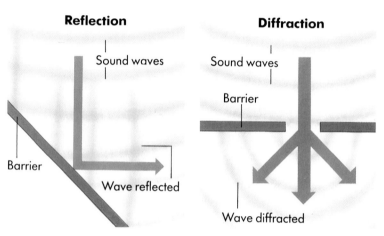

Reflection

Sound waves

Barrier

Wave reflected

Diffraction

Sound waves

Barrier

Wave diffracted

SEE FOR YOURSELF
If you take hold of the end of a length of rope and give it a quick up-and-down flick, a transverse wave will run along the rope. You can keep the waves going by keeping the end moving. You can also make waves by dropping a light ball into a bowl of water. The ripples that spread out are longitudinal waves.

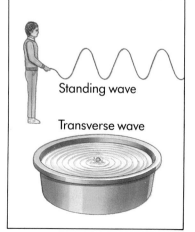

Standing wave

Transverse wave

---

passing a point each second is the FREQUENCY of the wave.

One important property of waves is that they can 'interfere'; if two waves are present in the same place at the same time, their effects add up. If the peaks of two equal waves arrive at a point at the same time, then they combine to give a peak twice as big. However, if the peaks of one wave arrive at an observer at the same time as the troughs of the other, they cancel each other out. Interference is important in DIFFRACTION, the way waves spread out as they pass through a narrow opening or around an obstacle.

See also REFLECTION; REFRACTION.

Wave motion

A wave motion is a pattern of disturbance that changes regularly as time passes and the wave moves from one place to another. The disturbance might be in the position of the surface of a liquid, as in waves on the sea, or in the PRESSURE of a gas, as in a SOUND wave in air, or in the electrical and magnetic fields, as in a LIGHT wave. Waves can be divided into travelling waves which move

◄ *A water droplet hitting the surface of water causes longitudinal waves that travel out in widening circles from where the drop landed. Two drops of water will each produce waves or ripples which will interfere with each other when they meet.*

along with time, like a sound wave in the open air, or standing waves which stay in the same place like the waves when a drum is struck. They can also be divided into longitudinal waves, such as sound in a FLUID, where the wave disturbance is in the same direction as the wave travels, and transverse waves such as light where the disturbance is at right angles to the direction of travel.
See also FREQUENCY; WAVE; WAVELENGTH.

Waves can also travel through solid material. If something is hit or twisted, it vibrates. The vibrations are waves that travel through the material. Earthquakes are waves travelling through solid rocks of the Earth. The denser the rocks, the faster the waves travel. Such waves can travel at several kilometres per second.

Wave power

Wave power describes the production of ELECTRICITY from the motion of waves at sea. As waves travel along the sea's surface, the water at any point on the surface does not travel with the wave. It moves up and down. This motion can be used to drive GENERATORS. Several types of wave-power generator have been designed and built. The best-known is the 'nodding duck'. A line of floats are each pivoted at one side, allowing the other side to nod up and down with the waves. The hub where each float pivots contains a dynamo to generate electricity directly or a water pump. The pump, driven by the nodding action of

Where the vibration is at right angles to the direction the wave is moving, the wave is a **transverse wave**. When the vibration is in the same direction as the direction of the wave, the wave is a **longitudinal wave**.

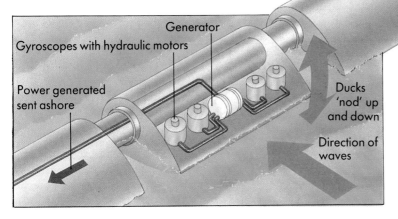

Generator
Gyroscopes with hydraulic motors
Power generated sent ashore
Ducks 'nod' up and down
Direction of waves

◄ *One method of generating power from sea waves uses rows of floats called nodding ducks. As the floats bob up and down, the energy in their movement is used to generate electricity.*

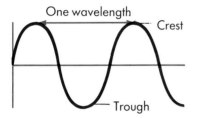

▲ *Wavelength is the distance between two waves.*

SEE FOR YOURSELF
To make a wax candle, tie a weight to some string passed through a hole in the bottom of a small carton. Tie the upper end of the string to a pencil, as shown. Carefully melt some wax crayons or ends of candles in an old pan on a gentle heat and pour the wax into the carton. Tear away the carton when the wax has set.

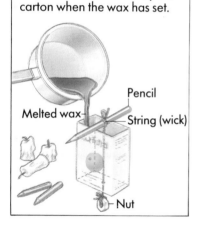

▼ *Honeybees make wax to build the comb in which they raise their grubs inside the hive.*

the float, pumps water through the float. The flow of this pumped water is used to power a TURBINE which drives a generator.
See also ENERGY; TIDAL POWER.

Wavelength

A wave is a disturbance that repeats itself in space; the wavelength is the distance between two similar places on the wave at one TIME; for example, it is the distance between one wave peak and the next. The wavelength, multiplied by the FREQUENCY of the wave, gives the wave's VELOCITY. This means that if two different sorts of ELECTROMAGNETIC RADIATION travel at the same velocity, the waves with higher frequency have shorter wavelengths and the waves with lower frequency have longer wavelengths. For example, a RADIO wave might have a frequency of 200 kHz (a kHz is one thousand cycles per second) and a wavelength of 1500 m, while a light wave might have a frequency of 600 THz (600 million million hertz) and a wavelength of 500 nm (500 millionths of a millimetre). Both have the same wave velocity.

Wax

A wax is a solid or semi-solid substance obtained from living things or from MINERAL sources. Examples include beeswax from the honeycomb of a beehive; tallow made from suet, which is the FAT inside animals such as cattle and sheep; and paraffin wax made from crude oil. Waxes are characterized by being insoluble in water, and by softening or melting when heated. Today synthetic waxes are manufactured by the PLASTICS industry. Waxes repel water and have many uses. They are used to coat paper and leather to make them waterproof. They are also made into furniture polishes, candles, crayons, cosmetics and ointments, and used in making matches and electrical INSULATORS.

Weather

Weather is the name given to the combination of the changing conditions of the ATMOSPHERE, including temperature, PRECIPITATION, atmospheric pressure, HUMIDITY, hours of sunshine, the amount and type of CLOUDS, and the speed and direction of the WIND. In some parts of

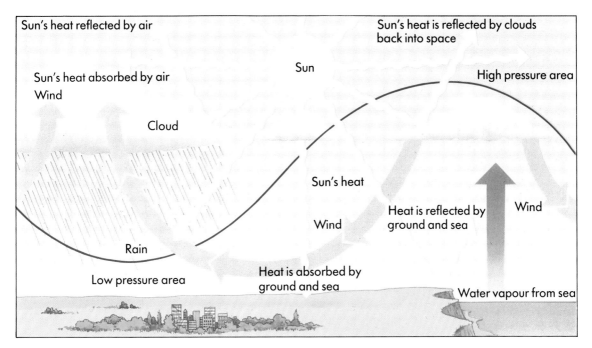

Sun's heat reflected by air

Sun's heat is reflected by clouds back into space

Sun

High pressure area

Sun's heat absorbed by air

Wind

Cloud

Sun's heat

Wind

Heat is reflected by ground and sea

Wind

Rain

Low pressure area

Heat is absorbed by ground and sea

Water vapour from sea

the world, such as western Australia, the weather may be the same week after week and month after month. Elsewhere, in areas such as the British Isles, the weather is very unstable, and may change from hour to hour; areas only a few miles apart may have different weather.

Weather is not the same as CLIMATE. Climate is the average weather of an area over a long period of time. The weather of a country such as Britain is changeable because the islands are located at a part of the globe where many different air masses (a large volume of air in which the temperature and humidity remain much the same as the air travels) may meet. The boundary between two different air masses is called a FRONT and it is these fronts, moving across a region, which give rise to the type of weather.

▲ *Weather is produced by the heat of the Sun and the effects it has on the atmosphere. The Sun's heat causes water to evaporate. The water vapour forms clouds in the atmosphere, which give rain or snow. Heat from the Sun warms the air, which rises, creating areas of low pressure. Wind is air moving from high-pressure areas to low-pressure areas.*

Weather Facts
The heaviest **rainstorm** occurred on the Indian Ocean Island of Réunion; in 1952 had 1870mm of rain in 24 hours. The driest place on Earth is Arica in Chile which averages only 0.76mm of rain per year. The highest **temperature** recorded was 58°C in the shade in Libya in 1922. The lowest temperature was −89.2°C at Vostok in Antarctica in 1983. The strongest surface **wind** was 372km/h recorded at Mt Washington in the United States in 1934.

Weather forecasting *See* Meteorology

Weathering *See* Erosion and Weathering

Weight

Weight is the downward FORCE which acts on all objects because they are attracted by GRAVITY towards the centre of the EARTH. The weight of an object depends on its MASS; an object with twice the mass has twice the weight, so an object's weight can be used to measure its

SEE FOR YOURSELF
Weight is a force. You can prove this by using a spring balance to weigh an object such as a banana. Weigh it in air and then weigh it again submerged in water. It weighs less in water because the water exerts an upward force (upthrust) that effectively lessens the force of gravity. The amount of upthrust is equal to the weight of water displaced by the banana.

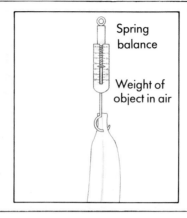

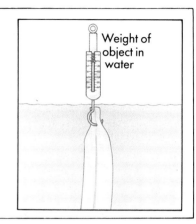

▶ *The mass of an object is constant but its weight depends on the force of gravity. 1 A person who weighs 120 kg on Earth weighs only 20 kg on the Moon 2, because the Moon's gravity is one-sixth of Earth's. The same person in a spaceship accelerating through space would weigh even less and would feel weightless 3.*

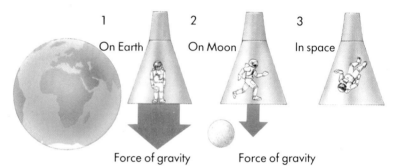

SEE FOR YOURSELF
Can you judge an object's weight by its size? It is not always possible. Of these 3 objects, the football is the largest but it is also the lightest. The brick, the smallest, is the heaviest. This is because the objects have very different densities. Only if objects have the same density are their sizes a guide to their weights.

mass. However, the mass and the weight are not the same; the mass depends only on the amount of material in the object and would be the same no matter where the object was taken in the Universe. The weight, however, depends on which other masses are nearby. For example, at the surface of the Moon the weight of an object is about one-sixth of its weight on the Earth because the force of gravity on the MOON is much less than that on Earth. Astronauts in a spacecraft orbiting the Earth feel no weight, because the pull of gravity causes them and their spacecraft to accelerate together towards the centre of the Earth. This is just like the sudden lessening in your weight that you feel when you stand in a lift which starts to move downwards.

Weights and Measures

Life around us depends greatly on being able to measure something accurately and meaningfully. Think of all the different things that you do that require some form of MEASUREMENT. Going on a journey requires a knowledge of distance and time, buying a carpet requires a knowledge of area, drawing a triangle requires a knowledge of angles, etc. But it is not just the measuring that is

◄ The best way of selling similar things of different sizes is by weight. Simple balances like this one have been used for thousands of years to weigh objects for sale.

important, it is the use of the most sensible units that matters. You would not measure the distance between two towns using a 30 cm ruler, but you might if the two towns were on a MAP.

Sometimes a choice of two units of measurement exists because we can directly relate the two units. For example, a 1 cm cube will hold 1 ml of water so we can measure volume and capacity in either cubic centimetres or millilitres.

Scientists throughout the world use the same units of length, time, mass and so on. These are called SI UNITS after the French for International System of Units. Using this system, a scientific measurement made in one country will use the same units as elsewhere.

Measuring Things
Everyday things are measured in only a few different units, such as millimetres and metres (for length), grams and kilograms (for mass), and millilitres and litres (for liquid volume). Which of these would be best to measure the following:
The length of a room?
The amount of fuel in a car's petrol tank?
The mass of a pencil?
The mass of a car?
The amount of medicine in a small bottle?
The length of a match?

Weismann, A. *See* Chromosomes and Genes

Welding

Welding is used to join METAL objects by melting their edges so that they fuse together. There are several welding methods: forge welding, OXYACETYLENE WELDING, ELECTRIC ARC welding, seam welding and spot welding. In forge welding, the parts are heated and then hammered together. Oxyacetylene welding uses a gas flame to heat the parts. In electric arc welding, the metal forms one electrode of an electric CIRCUIT and a metal rod called a filler rod forms the second electrode. When the two electrodes are held close together a spark jumps

▲ Building workers use oxyacetylene torches to cut and weld steel girders. Joints in sheet metal, such as for car body repairs, are usually made by electric arc welding.

▲ *George Westinghouse is best known for his invention of the air brake used in railway locomotives and vehicles.*

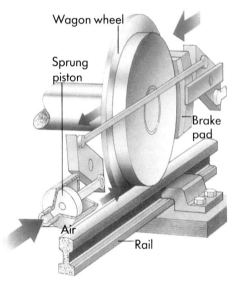

Wagon wheel

Sprung piston

Brake pad

Air

Rail

▲ *The Westinghouse brake uses air pressure to move a piston against the pressure of a spring. Movement of the piston works a lever that forces the brake pad against the edge of the wheel.*

▶ *A white dwarf is a star in the final stage of its life. A medium-sized star, like our Sun, gradually swells as it ages to become a red giant. The giant's outer material escapes into space, and its core shrinks to form a white dwarf.*

754

from one to the other, melting both the metal parts and the filler rod. Spot and seam welding are both electrical methods. The joint is clamped between two electrodes and a current passed through it. The electrical RESISTANCE of the metal causes it to heat up until it melts.

Westinghouse, George

George Westinghouse (1846–1914) was the US inventor and industrialist responsible for the use of alternating current (a.c.) for electrical supply in the United States. Westinghouse imported an a.c. system from Britain and developed it further. He employed the engineer Nikola Tesla to perfect it. After a struggle between a.c. and d.c. supporters, a.c. was eventually adopted.

In the 1860s Westinghouse produced a series of INVENTIONS ranging from a rotary STEAM ENGINE to his first major invention in 1869, the air brake. The Westinghouse air brake was widely used by railways in the United States. He went on to improve the design so that it worked automatically. He later developed a new railway signalling system and then patented several dozen original ideas for piping NATURAL GAS.

White dwarf

A white dwarf is the final stage of a normal STAR like our SUN, before it fades into blackness. It is the remains of the star's core, where the NUCLEAR ENERGY that made the star shine was generated. A white dwarf is made when a RED GIANT collapses at its centre. Although made of hydrogen and helium, which we know as gases, the atoms in a white dwarf are compressed so tightly that they are hundreds of times denser than lead. The surface is about 8000°C, but white dwarfs are so small they send out little light, and so are very hard to detect.

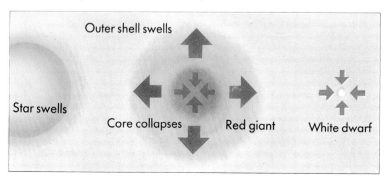

Star swells

Outer shell swells

Core collapses

Red giant

White dwarf

Whittle, Frank *See* Jet propulsion

Wind

Wind is the movement of AIR which depends upon variations in atmospheric PRESSURE. Air normally flows from areas of high atmospheric pressure to areas of low atmospheric pressure. In other words, if the EARTH did not spin on its axis, wind would normally blow from high to low pressure areas. But because the planet spins from west to east the winds are deflected to the right in the Northern HEMISPHERE and to the left in the Southern Hemisphere. This is called the Coriolis effect and, in the North, it means that the airflow is clockwise around an area of high pressure and anti-clockwise around an area of low pressure and in the South, the other way round.

The speed of the wind depends on the differences in the air pressures. If you look at a weather map, the winds

▲ *Trees that grow in places where there is a strong wind that usually comes from one direction grow crookedly, leaning away from the wind. The wind on the seashore usually comes from the sea.*

Beaufort Wind Scale
The force of the wind can be expressed on the Beaufort wind scale, which defines wind strength in terms of the wind's effects on objects in its path. The scale was devised by the British admiral Sir Francis Beaufort in 1805. The Beaufort scale is a series of numbers from 0 (no wind) to 12 (a violent hurricane). The steps on the scale are:
0 Calm (less than 1.6 km/h). Smoke rises straight up.
1–3 Light wind (up to 29 km/h). Leaves and twigs move, flags blow out.
4–5 Moderate wind (up to 38.6 km/h). Small trees sway, waves on lakes.
6–7 Strong wind (up to 61 km/h). Large trees sway, and walking is hard.
8–9 Gale (up to 87 km/h). Slates fall off roofs.
10–11 Storm (up to 116 km/h). Widespread damage is caused to buildings and property.
12 Hurricane (over 117 km/h). Disaster.

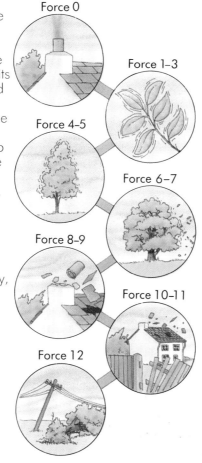

Force 0

Force 1–3

Force 4–5

Force 6–7

Force 8–9

Force 10–11

Force 12

▼ *The general directions of winds around the world follow a simple pattern. The directions of these winds is affected by the motion of the Earth spinning on its axis. They tend to blow in a south-westerly direction in the Northern Hemisphere and north-westerly in the Southern Hemisphere. There is little wind in the doldrums on either side of the equator.*

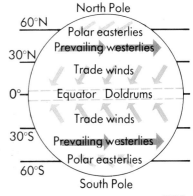

North Pole
60°N
Polar easterlies
Prevailing westerlies
30°N
Trade winds
0° Equator Doldrums
Trade winds
30°S
Prevailing westerlies
Polar easterlies
60°S
South Pole

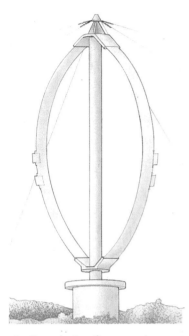

▲ *One design for a modern windmill has two curved blades that spin on a vertical axis. Strong cables act as guy ropes to anchor the mill and keep it upright.*

▶ *Windmills called bonnet mills, which have a 'cap' that moves round so that the sails always face the wind, were once common in the Fens of eastern England and in the Netherlands. Most of them were used for pumping water, not for grinding corn.*

will be strongest where the ISOBARS (lines of equal pressure) are closer together. Wind speed is measured using an ANEMOMETER. The speed or force of the wind may be measured by a scale of numbers from 1 to 12. This is referred to as the Beaufort scale.

Wind power

Wind power describes the ways in which the ENERGY of the WIND can be harnessed, usually to generate ELECTRICITY. It is one of the various kinds of alternative energy sources. One of the benefits of wind power is that it generates energy without any POLLUTION.

In flat countries such as the Netherlands, where the wind can blow without interruption, people have used windmills to grind their corn or to pump water from the ground for many years. Some countries, such as Britain, build very large wind generators, where one GENERATOR

SEE FOR YOURSELF
You can make a windmill from thin card. Cut out a four-pointed star as shown, making sure that the hole is exactly in the middle. Fold over the edges to form vanes, and use a drawing pin to fix the card to a wooden handle. Either fix the windmill upright in the ground or on a post, or swing it around at arm's length to create a flow of air over the vanes.

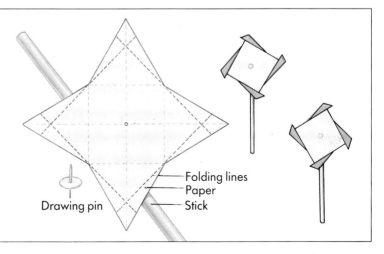

Folding lines
Paper
Drawing pin
Stick

◄ A collection of modern windmills make up a 'wind farm' in California, United States. The windmills drive generators that produce electricity.

can generate enough electricity for the local people in rural areas like the Shetland Islands. In other places 'wind farms' of many smaller windmills are constructed in isolated open areas. These 'farms' may include dozens of smaller windmills on tall towers.

Wind tunnel

A wind tunnel is a device used to study the way that AIR flows around objects. Powerful engines generate a constant flow of air through the tunnel and around test objects inside it. Sensors attached to the objects reveal whether the airflow is smooth or turbulent and measures forces such as lift and drag generated by the airflow.

Aircraft manufacturers test models of new aircraft in wind tunnels as do car manufacturers with models or full-size cars because streamlined vehicles use less FUEL. Architects test models of bridges and buildings to make sure that they are stable in high winds.

▲ The most efficient modern wind machines have two or three blades like the propeller of an aircraft. An electricity generator is located inside the 'head' of the machine. The head can also rotate to keep the blades pointed into the wind.

◄ A model of a Tornado jet fighter aircraft is tested in a wind tunnel to observe the effects on its aerodynamics caused by hanging missiles and extra fuel tanks underneath it.
If the aircraft is to carry heavy missiles it will need extra fuel, but it can only carry a certain amount of weight so it must be made as streamlined as possible.

▲ *A cable contains many wires, all carrying different currents. Cables such as this are commonly used for carrying communications signals, such as telephone messages. Each separate wire in the cable is surrounded by insulating material, which is usually plastic. This is to stop the current from jumping from wire to wire.*

All wood decay is caused by bacteria and fungi. They eat into the cells and leave rotting wood behind. If they were deprived of oxygen, heat and moisture, they could not exist and the wood would last indefinitely. Some piles that Julius Caesar used in bridges in France were found to be sound after 2000 years.

▶ *The wood in a tree trunk forms in layers which appear as rings if the trunk is cut through. Beneath the outer bark is a layer of sapwood containing rings of phloem and xylem vessels. These are made up of tiny tubes and run the length of the trunk to carry food and water to the branches and leaves. A new ring of wood is formed each year and so it is possible to tell the age of a tree by counting the rings. The hard dry centre of the trunk is called heartwood.*

The largest wind tunnel in the world is operated by the US space agency, NASA, in California, USA, and its six engines can produce air speeds of up to 555 km/h. *See also* AERODYNAMICS; STREAMLINING.

Wire

Wire is a flexible, fine strand of metal. A cable made from a number of metal strands twisted together is also called wire. Wire for electrical purposes is made from a good CONDUCTOR of electricity such as copper.

The electrical conductor is usually covered with a coating of plastic or enamel called a sleeve to insulate it from other conductors. A cable may contain a number of individual wires, each with its own plastic sleeve. The plastic sleeves may be colour-coded to identify which wire does what in a CIRCUIT. Mains electrical wiring, for example, is coded so that it can be connected correctly and safely to plugs and household appliances.

Wire is made by pulling metal rods through a series of progressively smaller holes in metal blocks called dies in a process called drawing.

Wood

Wood is the tough material that forms trunks and branches of trees. The same material also occurs in smaller amounts in the ROOTS and STEMS of other plants. It consists of tough-walled tubes and fibres in the plant's xylem. The tubes carry water and mineral salts up the trunk to the LEAVES, while the fibres provide the additional strength necessary to support the trunk and branches. The tubes and fibres start out as living CELLS, but a CARBOHYDRATE called lignin soon begins to build

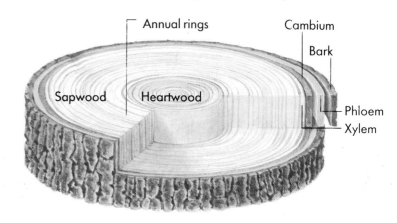

Annual rings · Cambium · Bark · Sapwood · Heartwood · Phloem · Xylem

up in their walls and make them hard. The cells then die, although they still work in the same way.

A tree trunk grows thicker by producing a new ring of wood just under the bark every year. The rings are clearly marked in trees growing in cool regions, where growth stops in the winter. They are called annual rings and are less obvious in tropical trees, which generally grow throughout the year. The oldest wood in the centre of the trunk gradually gets crushed and cannot carry water. It is called heartwood and is usually harder and darker than the wood on the outside. This younger wood, which still carries water, is called sapwood.

Large areas of the world used to be covered with trees but nowadays they are being cut down for FUEL, to make PAPER and to clear land for farming.

See also DEFORESTATION; DENDROCHRONOLOGY.

Word processor

A word processor is a COMPUTER designed to be used for creating, editing and storing text. At any time, the text may be retrieved from the word processor's memory and printed. A word processor consists of a keyboard similar to a typewriter keyboard, a VISUAL DISPLAY UNIT for displaying the text, a computer dedicated to processing text, a memory device such as a disk drive and a printer. The disk drive stores the text on magnetic disks until it is needed again. A microcomputer with a word-processing program can be used as a word processor.

Text is entered on the keyboard. After it has been

▼ In many offices that deal with large amounts of text, several word processors can be linked to a central data bank as a network. In a network, several word processors can use the same printer and scanning system for reading text.

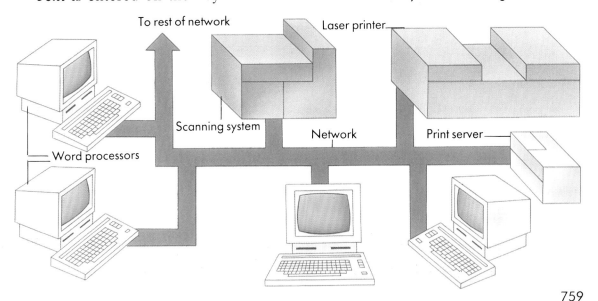

To rest of network

Laser printer

Scanning system

Network

Print server

Word processors

759

Work is done

Work is not done

▲ *Work is done when a force makes something move in the direction of the force. Pushing a car along involves work, but holding a book does not because the book is not being moved.*

▼ *In a steam locomotive, work is done by steam pressure because it makes the pistons move. The heat energy of the steam is converted into the mechanical energy of the moving piston. But some energy is wasted as work that has to be done to overcome friction in the moving parts.*

entered, it can be changed, corrected and moved about on the screen before printing. Some word processors can incorporate graphics to produce illustrated documents. *See also* COMPUTER GRAPHICS; HARDWARE; SOFTWARE.

Work

In PHYSICS, work is said to be done when an object on which a FORCE is acting moves in the direction of that force. For example, if you are helping to push a car from the back and the car moves forward, you do work on the car. On the other hand, if you are standing holding a heavy book still in your hands, you do not do any work on it since the book is not moving. Similarly, if you are pushing the car from the side, even if the car moves forwards (not sideways), you do not do any work because the car did not move in the same direction that you were pushing.

Work is the way in which ENERGY is changed from one form into another; having a certain amount of energy means that you are able to do a certain amount of work. Work and energy are both measured in JOULES. For example, when pushing the car, chemical energy stored in your body goes into doing work, which increases the kinetic energy of the car. Machines are designed to make the best use of the work that is done by reducing the FRICTION forces, the amount of kinetic energy lost, or wasted, as HEAT and so on.

▶ *The work done in using a spanner is equal to the force applied to the handle multiplied by the distance the handle moves in the direction of the force.*

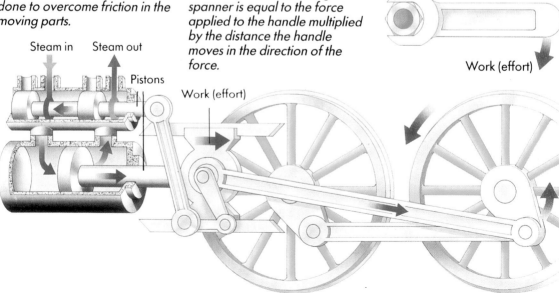

Steam in   Steam out

Pistons

Work (effort)

Work (effort)

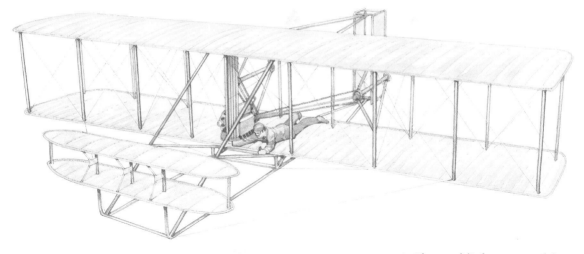

▲ *The world's first successful powered aeroplane, Flyer I* (above) *was built after experimenting with gliders* (left).

Wright, Orville and Wilbur

Wilbur Wright (1867–1912) and his brother Orville (1871–1948) made the world's first controlled flight of a powered aeroplane in 1903. The two brothers were interested in machines and designed and made printing presses and then bicycles.

Between 1900 and 1902 they built a series of gliders to test the controls that would be used in their next venture, the powered aeroplane called Flyer I. Its historic flight on 17 December 1903 at Kill Devil Hills, Kitty Hawk, in the US state of North Carolina lasted 12 seconds. They went on to build more aeroplanes, improving the design each time. They had to design and make their own propellers and ENGINES because none that was suitable existed at the time. Wilbur demonstrated their aeroplanes in Europe in 1908 and 1909. Meanwhile, Orville built the first military aeroplane for the US Army. *See also* FLIGHT.

▲ *The Wright brothers, Wilbur* (top) *and Orville* (bottom) *played an important part in the development of aircraft.*

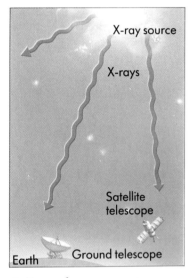

▲ *X-rays from sources in space cannot be detected by telescopes on Earth. The first satellite to carry X-ray detectors was launched by the Soviet Union in 1958.*

Xerography *See* Photocopier

X-ray astronomy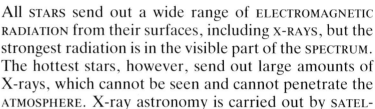

All STARS send out a wide range of ELECTROMAGNETIC RADIATION from their surfaces, including X-RAYS, but the strongest radiation is in the visible part of the SPECTRUM. The hottest stars, however, send out large amounts of X-rays, which cannot be seen and cannot penetrate the ATMOSPHERE. X-ray astronomy is carried out by SATELLITES, such as ROSAT, launched in 1990.

To produce X-rays in a star, temperatures of at least a million degrees are needed. The Sun's core (about 15 million °C) produces them, and they would gradually destroy our CELLS if the atmosphere did not protect us.

There are many very bright X-ray objects in the sky: SUPERNOVAE, WHITE DWARFS, QUASARS, and NEUTRON STARS all send out X-rays. Some PULSARS also emit them, as do BLACK HOLES such as Cygnus X-1.

X-ray diffraction

X-ray diffraction is used to discover how the ATOMS of a CRYSTAL are arranged. The atoms of a crystal lie in orderly rows. The spaces between the rows bend, or diffract, beams of X-rays. In 1912 the German physicist Max von Laue used a crystal to diffract X-rays, for which he received the NOBEL Prize for Physics in 1914. The pattern of intense spots made on photographic film by diffracted X-rays gives information about the crystal's structure. The relationship between the spots and the

Sir William Henry Bragg (1862–1942) and Sir William Lawrence Bragg (1890–1971)
The Braggs, father (left) and son, were British physicists who developed the technique of X-ray diffraction to investigate crystals. When they aimed a beam of X-rays at a crystal, the regular arrangement of atoms in the crystal scattered the X-rays to produce a characteristic pattern on a photographic plate. They shared the 1915 Nobel Prize in Physics.

spacing of atoms in the crystal was discovered by the two physicists, William and Lawrence Bragg. X-ray diffraction was used by Crick, Watson and Wilkins to find the structure of the genetic material, DNA.

X-rays

X-rays are one kind of ELECTROMAGNETIC RADIATION. They have a very high FREQUENCY of about a million million million hertz (cycles per second), and so a very short WAVELENGTH. They were discovered in 1895 by Wilhelm Roentgen; he gave them their name because the letter X is often used to stand for something unknown. Materials which contain only light atoms do not absorb many X-rays. For example, they pass easily through most living tissue, but not through BONES which contain heavier atoms. This means that X-rays can be used to find what is wrong with bones and teeth inside the body without surgery. Because X-rays are a form of ionizing RADIATION, which can damage cells, the amount that a person receives has to be carefully controlled. X-rays are used to study the structure of SOLIDS in X-RAY DIFFRACTION, and in X-RAY ASTRONOMY.

X-rays can be produced by bombarding atoms with fast particles and knocking ELECTRONS out from the 'shells' near the middle of the atom. Other electrons move in from the outer shells to take the place of the missing electrons, giving out ENERGY as X-rays.

▲ X-ray diffraction is used to work out the structure of complicated molecules. This pattern is produced by DNA, which makes up genes and chromosomes in the cell nucleus.

Wilhelm Conrad Roentgen (1845–1923)
Roentgen was a German physicist. In 1895 he noticed that rays from a covered cathode-ray tube (which would emit no cathode rays) caused a phosphorescent screen to fluoresce. He deduced that this was caused by a new type of radiation, which he called X-rays. For this work, he received the first Nobel Prize for Physics in 1901.

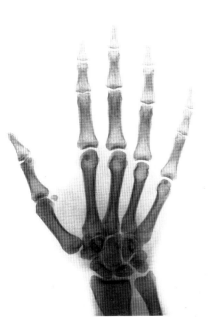

◀ Modern medical X-ray photographs, using carefully controlled doses of X-rays, can reveal the structure of soft tissues as well as hard tissues such as bone.

▼ X-rays form the part of the electromagnetic spectrum beyond ultraviolet rays. At very short wavelengths, they become gamma rays.

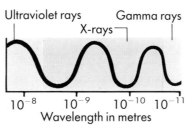

Ultraviolet rays   Gamma rays
          X-rays
10^{-8} 10^{-9} 10^{-10} 10^{-11}
Wavelength in metres

Yeast

Yeasts are tiny single-celled MICROORGANISMS that are part of the group called fungi. They reproduce asexually, by budding off tiny CELLS which grow and eventually reproduce themselves. Some yeasts live naturally on the body, and they may cause DISEASE, such as thrush also known as candida, which can affect the mouth and sex organs. Yeasts also grow naturally on the surface of FRUIT, feeding on the SUGARS the fruit contains.

Some yeasts are essential in the process of FERMENTATION. When these yeasts grow in the presence of sugar, they break the sugar down to produce ethanol, a simple ALCOHOL, and release carbon dioxide. We make use of this property in making alcoholic drinks like wine and beer, when the yeast ferments fruit sugars to make wine, or malt sugars present in grain to make beer. Yeast is also useful in baking, where the carbon dioxide gas it produces causes bread to rise. Yeast is a valuable source of PROTEIN and some VITAMINS of the B group, and it can be taken as yeast extract.

See also BIOTECHNOLOGY; GENETIC ENGINEERING.

Dough fermented with yeast is called *leaven*. The name comes from the Latin word meaning 'to raise', because fermented dough rises. Bread made of fermented dough is called leavened bread. The old English word for leaven is *yeast*.

SEE FOR YOURSELF
To watch yeast ferment, add a spoonful of sugar to a small jug of warm milk or water. Stir in some baker's yeast (or dried yeast), stand the jug on a tray and put it in a warm place. A few hours later the milk will froth over as the yeast breaks down the sugar to release carbon dioxide gas.

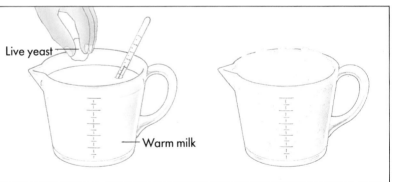

Live yeast

Warm milk

▶ *Seen using an electron microscope, baker's yeast is revealed as a single-celled fungus. It is used in making bread, where the carbon dioxide produced by fermentation makes the bread rise. Yeast is also used in the production of beer and wine, in which it converts the sugar from the fruit, hops or barley into carbon dioxide and alcohol.*

Zinc

Zinc is a bluish-grey ELEMENT. It is a METAL, and has been known and used for hundreds of years. Its main use today is in GALVANIZING steel. The steel is covered with zinc either by being dipped or by ELECTROLYSIS to form a protective coating that prevents the steel from rusting. Galvanized steel is used in roofing and to make water tanks. Zinc is also used to make BATTERIES.

Zinc is a part of various ALLOYS, such as brass (zinc

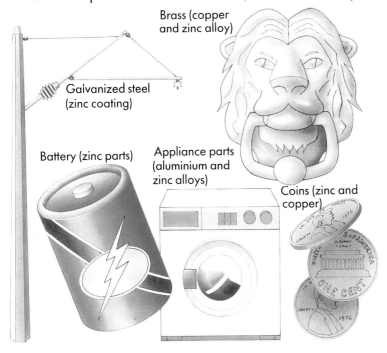

Brass (copper and zinc alloy)

Galvanized steel (zinc coating)

Battery (zinc parts)

Appliance parts (aluminium and zinc alloys)

Coins (zinc and copper)

◀ Zinc is a metal with many uses, chief of which is in galvanizing steel (as for the posts that hold up overhead wires for electric railways). It is also made into the outer cases of dry batteries. The chief zinc alloy is brass, although other alloys are used in machines and to make coins.

▲ Zinc is a metal element. Like most metals it is shiny in its pure form but is only found in nature as zinc compounds.

and copper) and the zinc-based alloy (with aluminium and copper) used for casting objects such as pots and door handles. Zinc oxide is the PIGMENT known as Chinese white and is used in antiseptic ointments. Zinc sulphide glows when hit by ULTRAVIOLET light or X-RAYS and is used to coat the inside of TELEVISION screens and in luminous dials on clocks.

See also CORROSION; IRON AND STEEL; LUMINESCENCE.

Zoology

Zoology is the study of animals, from amoeba and other single-celled protozoans to humans and the huge whales. It covers the structure of the animals and their internal workings as well as the way in which they behave and how they live. *See* pages 766 and 767.

Zinc was used by the Romans more than 2000 years ago, but because it is always found in combination with other elements, it was not identified as a separate metal until the 1500s by the Swiss doctor Paracelsus.

ZOOLOGY

Zoology is a very large subject because there are over a million known animal species living everywhere on the Earth. Most zoologists specialize in one particular topic, such as physiology, which is the study of the processes of the animals' lives including their respiration, how they get rid of waste, how they reproduce and so on. Others may study a particular group of animals. Entomologists, for example, study insects and ornithologists study birds. Many entomologists are involved with the control of insect pests, such as mosquitoes and locusts. Many other zoologists work in agriculture and in veterinary medicine, breeding animals for our farms and learning how to prevent and cure their various illnesses.

Ecology deals with the ways in which animals fit into their environments. It is very important for us to find out exactly what conditions the animals need if we are to conserve them in the wild. Sometimes animal species are threatened in their natural habitat and so a small population of them is preserved in a zoo or wildlife park. Some countries have game reserves or large national parks set aside for animals to live in without the interference of humans.

▲ *Some of the smallest of the world's animals make up the plankton that lives on and near the surface of the seas. This sample includes minute copepods and the larvae of crustaceans such as crabs and shrimps. Marine plankton are the starting point for a huge number of food chains. Many fish and birds eat plankton. Even some whales exist by sieving huge quantities of minute plankton from the Antarctic waters.*

▼ *There are more than 80,000 species of birds in the world, from flightless penguins to high-flying vultures, and aquatic ducks and geese.*

▼ *Frogs are amphibians. Like toads, newts and salamanders, they lay their eggs in water but their tadpole-like larvae change into land animals.*

▼ *The Blue whale is a mammal that lives in the sea and is the world's largest animal. It may grow to more than 30 metres in length and weigh over 100 tonnes.*

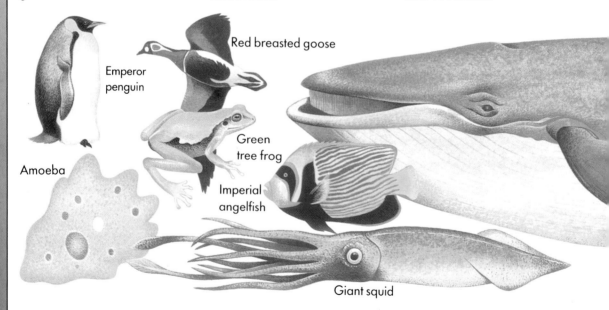

Emperor penguin

Red breasted goose

Green tree frog

Amoeba

Imperial angelfish

Giant squid

▲ *An amoeba is a microscopic single-celled animal whose jelly-like body engulfs its food and pulls it inside to digest it. There are many other microscopic animals*

▲ *Fishes are the largest group of backboned animals (vertebrates), with about 20,000 different species varying in size from a few millimetres to 12 metres.*

▲ *The Giant squid is the largest of the animals without backbones (invertebrates). It is a cephalopod which grows up to 15 metres long (including its tentacles).*

▶ Zoologists study the territories of birds, their population changes and how they migrate by ringing them. Here a Sedge warbler is having a ring put on its leg. Each ring carries the address of the national organization that coordinates the information about birds that are found. A record card is filled in for each bird ringed with its weight, wing length and species and the card is sent to the national organization and kept in case the bird is caught or found again.

Zoologists are always making fascinating discoveries. Until recently it was thought that insects blundered into spiders' webs by accident. But it was found recently that some spiders' webs reflect ultraviolet light which attracts insects to them.

▼ The Goliath beetle is the size of a man's fist and is one of the heaviest insects in the world (some moths are larger). Insects are part of a larger group, the Arthropods.

SEE FOR YOURSELF
How many worms are there in a square metre of lawn? More than you think! To find out, use string to peg out a measured square metre and, towards sunset, water the grass with dilute washing-up liquid. This will bring the worms to the surface. When it is dark, go out with a torch and collect the worms in a bowl. Release them after you have counted them.

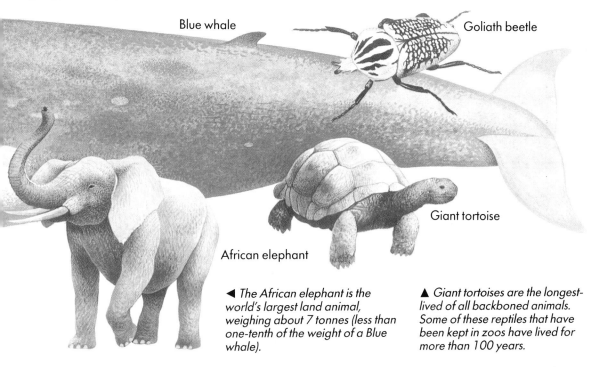

Blue whale

Goliath beetle

Giant tortoise

African elephant

◀ The African elephant is the world's largest land animal, weighing about 7 tonnes (less than one-tenth of the weight of a Blue whale).

▲ Giant tortoises are the longest-lived of all backboned animals. Some of these reptiles that have been kept in zoos have lived for more than 100 years.

See also AGRICULTURE; BIOLOGY; BOTANY; BREEDING; CLASSIFICATION; CONSERVATION, ENVIRONMENTAL; ECOLOGY; ORGANISM; SPECIES.

Zygote

When an ovum or EGG cell is fertilized by a sperm, it produces a zygote. This single CELL holds genes from both parents, and contains all of the instructions needed to make a complete organism, with all its organs and structure pre-planned. The human zygote, for example, holds genes such as those which determine if the child will have blue or brown eyes, or dark or fair hair.

The zygote stays as one cell for only a very short time, because it begins to divide and this quickly leads to the next stage in development, called a blastula.

It is a zygote which is produced by test-tube FERTILIZATION when helping couples who have been unsuccessful in having children. The sperm fertilizes an ovum which has been removed from a woman's ovary. The blastula, consisting of several cells, is implanted back into the woman to continue its development normally.

▼ A zygote forms when the nuclei of two sex cells (one male, the sperm and one female, the egg) join at fertilization. Once one sperm penetrates the egg, the egg's outer membrane thickens to prevent any more sperm from entering.

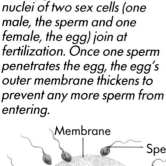

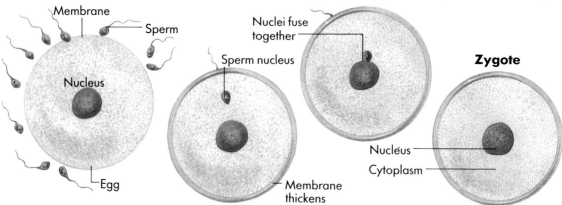

▶ A crowd of human sperm, (coloured blue), try to penetrate the outer membrane of an egg, (coloured yellow). The sperm look roughly spherical because their long tails do not show up on this electron microscope photograph. If a sperm gets through, fertilization takes place and the zygote formed eventually develops into a new individual.

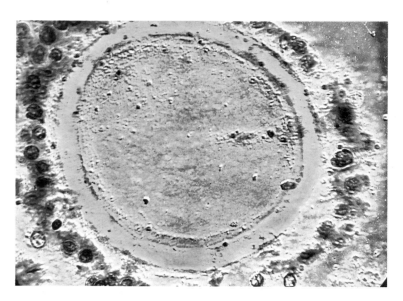

About Your Index

This index has been designed to help you find which articles will have information on the subject you are looking up. You may find that although there is no article on your subject, for example Aircraft, you will find a lot of information about it in other articles, such as Aerodynamics, Flight, Jet propulsion and the Wright brothers.

The page numbers listed in this index are of different types. Those printed in **bold type** indicate where the main entry for the subject can be found, whereas page numbers in *italic type* refer to pages on which illustrations will be found. When you look

up Acids and Bases, for example, you will see:

Acids and Bases 4, *4*
litmus 347, 407
pH 533, *533*

The main entry on this subject is on page 4 where there is also an illustration. Further information can be found under the articles on Litmus and pH.

After the main index you will find a Subject Index. In this, all the articles in the encyclopedia are divided up by subject. The entries are in alphabetical order within each subject. In addition there is an index of entries which are Special Features.

A

Abacus 1, *1*, 50
Abel, Frederick 724
Aberdeen Angus cattle *82*
Abrasives 1, *1*, 307
Absolute zero *see* **Kelvin**
Absorption 2
sound waves 5
Acceleration 2–3, *2*
inertia 351
mass 429
terminal velocity 695
velocity 729
Accelerometer 351
Accumulator 56
Acetone *see* Propanone
Acetylene 514–515, *515*
Acid rain 3, *3*, 156, 558, 674
Acids and Bases 4, *4*
litmus 347, 407
pH 533, *533*
Acoustics 4–5, 541
Acre 436
Acrilan 684
Acrophobia 572
Adams, John Couch 324, 482, *482*
Adaptation 6
Addiction, to tranquillizers 708–709
Additives, food 256–257, *257*
Adelard of Bath 499
Adenoids *415*
Adenovirus *735*
Adhesives 7, *7*
epoxy resins 220–221, *220*, 548
Adler (aircraft designer) 250
Adolescence 7–8, *8*, 300
Adrenal glands 328, 665
Adrenaline 328
Aeoliphile 318, *318*
Aerial 28–29, *28*
Aerial photography:
map-making 424
stereoscopic 664
Aerobic respiration 593
Aerodynamics 8–10, *8–10*, *541*, 668
Aerofoils 8
Aeroplane *see*
Aircraft; **Flight** etc

Aerosols 10, *10*, 466
chlorofluorocarbons 116
colloids 131
Africa:
continent 152
monsoon 469
peoples *544*
African elephant *767*
Agar *526*
Aging 10–11
Agoraphobia 572
Agriculture 12, *12*
fertilizers *23*, 24
genetics 285
irrigation 370, *370*
pesticides 530–531, *530–531*
veterinary medicine *731*, 732
water pollution 558
AIDS 13, *13*
and immune system 346, 735
Air 13–15, *14–15*
aerodynamics 8–10, *8–10*
aqualungs 32–33, *32*
atmosphere 42–43
composition *14*
compressors 140, *140*
environment 218
evaporation 225
as a fluid *253*
hovercraft 330
humidity 331–332, *332*, 342
as a liquid 406
pneumatics 553–554, *553*
resistance 3
weather fronts 270–271
wind 755–756, *755*
Air conditioning 16, *16*, 315
evaporation 224–225
heat pumps 311
humidifiers 331
Air cushion vehicle *see*
Hovercraft
Air pollution 14, **17**, *17*, 558, *558–559*
fog 256
sulphur dioxide 674
Air pressure 14, *14*, 566
and boiling point 76
cyclones 163
Aircraft:
aerodynamics 8–9, *8–9*
aluminium alloys *21*
autopilots 38

carbon fibres *95*
contrails *146*
engines 217
flight 250, *250*, 253
hydraulics *334*
inertial guidance 351, *351*
jet propulsion 374, *374–375*
Mach number 417, *417*, 638
radar 578, *578*
sound barrier 640, *640*
supersonic 678–679, *678–679*
wind tunnels 757, *757*
Wright brothers 761, *761*
Airships 250
Alabaster 672
Alaska:
maps 425
oil pollution 559
Albino *544*
Alchemy 18, *18*, 114
Alcohol 19, *19*
antifreeze 30
as an antiseptic 32
as a drug 185
fermentation 242, 764
liver disease 408
as a solvent 636
thermometers 235, 697–698
Aldebaran *587*
Aldrin, Edwin 40
Algae 127, *455*
chemical indicator 347
green algae *78*
lichen 681, *681*
water pollution 487
Algebra 19–20, *20*, 432
Aliphatic hydrocarbons 335
Alkali 4
pH 533, *533*
litmus 347, 407
Alkaline battery 56
Alkanes 335, 532
octane 504
paraffin 521
propane 570
Alkenes *335*, 532
Allergy 20–21, *20*
to food 500
Alloy 21, *21*, 445
amalgam 23
copper 155
zinc 765
Alpha Centauri 571, *571*

Alpha radiation 236, 582, *582*
Alpine swift *668*
Alps 473
Alternating current (a.c.) 202, *202*, 754
diode 179
rectifier 586, *586*
Alternative medicine 435
Alternator 283, *283*
Altocumulus cloud *129*
Altostratus cloud *129*
Aluminium 22, *22*, *444*
alloys *21*
anodizing 28
Aluminium oxide 514
Alveolus *413*, 414
Amalgam 23, *23*
Amanita pantherina
toadstool *554*
American Academy of Arts and Sciences 604
American Association for the Advancement of Science 604
American Civil War (1861–65) 487
American Revolution (1775–83) 596, 670
Amide 561
Amino acids 561, 570, *570*
Ammeters 24
Ammonia 23–24, *23–24*, *221*, 341, *531*
in animal waste 488
fertilizers 244
fountain experiment *356*
molecules 467
in solution 635
Ammonites 232
Ammonium chloride 56
Ammonium nitrate 704
Amoeba 66, 102, *766*
Ampere 24, 159, 452, 619
Ampère, André 24, *24*
Amphibians 126
evolution 227
extinction *232*
heart *310*
hibernation 319
larvae 388
lungs 413–414
Amplifier 25, *25*
hi-fi 320
Amplitude *638*, 747, *747*
Amplitude modulation (AM) 580, *580–581*

Diffraction **176–177**, *176–177*
  light 83, *83*
  waves 748, *748*

I

Ice **229**, *229*, 344, *344*
  dry ice 186, *186*
  dust particles *359*
  erosion *222*, 223
  freezing 267, 405, *745*
  glaciers *292–293*, 293
  hydrogen bonds 340
  precipitation 565
Ice Age 344, *344*
Icebergs *171*, 344, *344*, 637
Iceland, maps 425
Igneous rocks 345, *345*, 602, *602–603*
  formation 393
  metamorphic rocks 445–446
  mica 452
  ores 509
Ileum *see* **Intestine**
Illness *see* **Disease**
Immiscible, definition 466–467
Immune system 346, *346*
  AIDS 13
  antibiotics 29
  antibodies and antigens 30
  transplants 711–712
  vaccination 722, *722*
  viruses 735
Impeller 575
Impermeable, definition 37
Implode, definition 61
Implosion 346, *347*
Incidence, angle of 465
Incisor teeth 687, *687*
Inclined plane *416*
Incubators *435*
Index (mathematics) 433
India:
  early technology 688
  monsoon 469
  music 477
  plastic surgery 547
Indian Ocean 503
monsoon 469, *469*
Indicator, chemical 347, *347*
  acids and bases 4
  litmus 407, *407*
  pH 533
  titration 704
Inductance, self and magnetic 348, *348*
Induction, electric
  generators 282–283
Induction coil 349, *349*
Industrial Revolution 130, **349–350**, *349–350*, 417, 596, 688, *689*, 715
Industry:
  pollution 17, *17*, 558, 742
  robots 599
Inertia 350–351, *350–351*, 429
Inertial guidance 351, *351*, 465
Infection 180, **351–352**
  antiseptics 31–32
  definition 31
  immune system 346, *346*
  lymph system 414–415
Infectious, definition 180
Infinity 352, *352*, 498
Influenza 735
Information technology 353, *353*

Infrared astronomy 354, *354*
Infrared photography 354, *354*
Infrared radiation 206, *206*, **354–355**, *354*
  false-colour photography 236
  spectrum 652
Inheritance *see* **Heredity**
Injection moulding 355, *355*
Inoculation 722
Inorganic chemistry 356, *356*
  see also Chemistry Subject Index
Insecticide *226*, 530–531, *673*
Insects:
  antenna 28, *28*
  breathing 81
  camouflage 89, *89*
  ecosystem *195*
  hibernation 319
  larvae 388–389, *388*
  metamorphosis 446–447, *446–447*
  migration 459
  natural selection 480
  pigments 544
  pollination of flowers 557, *557*
  skeleton 622
Insoluble, definition 635
Instinct 58, **357**, *357*
Instruments, musical 357–358, *358*
  synthesizers 682–683, *683*
Instruments, scientific 359, *359*
Insulation:
  foam rubber 255
  thermal 360, *360*
Insulators, electrical 148, **361**, *361*
  alloys 21
  glass 294
Insulin:
  diabetes 180
  functions 328, *520*
  genetic engineering 284, *284*
  pancreas 294, 520, *520*
Integrated circuit 210, *210–211*, **361**, *362*
  calculators 86
  computers 142, 145
  microchips 454, *454*
  microprocessors 456, *456*
Intel Corporation 456
Intelligence 362
  artificial 38, *38*
Interference, wave 176, *176*, 748
Internal combustion engine 217, **362–363**, *363*, 689
  diesel 175–176, *176*
  fuel injection 275, *275*
  gas turbine 280–281, *280*
  induction coil 349
  Wankel engine 741, *741*
International Council of Scientific Unions (ICSU) 604
Internet 353
Interstellar matter 364, *364*
Intestine 178, **364**, *364*
Inuit 6
Invention 365, *365*

Invertebrates 622
Involuntary muscles 476
Io 378, *378*, 610
Iodides 365
Iodine 365, *365*
  halogen lamps 306
  as indicator of starch 655, *655*
  metamorphosis of tadpoles 446
  radioisotopes 373
  as trace element 707–708
Ion 366, *366*
  bonds 77
  mass spectroscopy *429*, 430
Ion propulsion 366, *366*
Ionization 366
Ionizing radiation 578, 763
Ionosphere 42, 190, **367**, *367*
  solar wind 631
  telecommunications 290, 579
Iridescence 367–368, *368*
Iridium 551
Iris *663*
Irish elk 226
Iron and Steel *115*, **368–369**, *369*, *444*
  alloys 21, 423–424
  blast furnaces 73–74, *73–74*
  cast iron 96
  in cereals 108
  expansion 229
  forging 262–263, *263*
  freezing point 268
  galvanizing 277–278
  melting point *438*
  rust (iron oxide) 156, *156*, 368, *513*, 514
  trace element 707–708
  valency 725
Iron chloride *635*
Irradiation 260, 261, **369–370**, *369–370*, 665
Irrigation *174*, 365, **370**, *370*
Iso, definition 371
Isobar 371, *371*
Isomer 371–372, *371*
Isometric, definition 371
Isosceles triangle 371, 560
Isotherm 372, *372*
Isotonic 372–373, *372*
  definition 371
Isotope 373, *373*, 484
  definition 371
  mass spectroscopy 429–430
  medical uses 583

J

Jacquard loom *350*
Japan:
  paper-making *520*
  robots 599
Java, tsunamis 700–701
Jellyfish 742
Jenner, Edward 323, 722, *722*
Jensen, Johannes Hans 571, *571*
Jet propulsion 280, 374, *374–375*
Jet stream 375, *375*
Jetfoil 337
Jewellery, gold 296
Jews, medicine 435

Joint, universal *198*
Joints 376, *376*, 623
  artificial hips 695
  lubrication 412
Joliot, Frederic 162
Joliot-Curie, Irene 162
Jolson, Al 122
Joule 216, 313, **377**, *377*, 382, 619
Joule, James Prescott 324, 377, *377*
Joule's law 377, *377*
Julian calendar 86
Juniper *405*
Juniperus communis 405
Jupiter 378, *378*, 632, *633*
  asteroids 39
  atmosphere 449
  escape velocity 224
  gravity 298
  moons 277, *277*, 609–610
  space probe 644, 645
Jurassic Period *227*, 232, *288*

K

Kalahari Desert 173
Kaleidoscope 379, *379*
Kangaroo *70*
Kaolin 562, *562*
Karst *603*
Keck telescope 693
Kekulé, August 60, 356
Kelly, Henry 368
Kelvin 380, *380*, 452, 619
Kelvin, William Thomson 377, **380**, *380*
Kelvin scale 105, *105*
Kennecott's Bingham Canyon mine *463*
Kennedy Space Center 646
Kepler, Johannes 41, 80, 158, 323, **380–381**, *380*
Keratin 239
Kerosene 507
Kettle lakes *293*
Kevlar *430*
Keys and Locks 409, *409*
Khayyam, Omar 19
Kidneys 75, 228, *228*, **381**, *381*
Kilimanjaro, Mount 712
Kiln 382, *382*
Kilocalorie 377
Kilogram 452, 619, *619*
Kiloherz 318
Kilojoule 313, 377, 501
Kilowatt-hour 382, *382*
Kim's Game *439*
Kinetic energy 216, *474*, *526*
Kinetoscope *196*
Kipp's apparatus *356*
Kirchhoff, Gustav Robert 148, *148*, 324, 545
Kirchhoff's laws 148
Knee joint 376, *376*
Knoll, Max 209
Koch, Robert 435, *435*, 453, 526
Kodak 537
Kokoi arrow-poison frog 554
Korea, paper-making *520*
Krakatoa 700–701, 738
Krypton 42, 402, 490–491
Kubasov, Valery 40

Subject Index

Astronomy

Asteroid
Astronaut
Astronomy
Aurora
Big Bang theory
Big Crunch theory
Binary stars
Black hole
Calendar
Comet
Constellation
Corona
Cosmic rays
Cosmology
Daylength
Eclipse
Expansion theory
Galaxy
Geostationary orbit
Globular clusters
Halley's comet
Infrared astronomy
Interstellar matter
Jupiter
Light year
Magellanic clouds
Mars
Mercury (planet)
Meteor
Meteorite
Milky Way galaxy
Moon
Nebula
Neptune
Neutron star
Nova
Orbit
Orrery
Parallax
Parsec
Planet
Planetarium
Pluto
Precession
Proxima Centauri
Pulsar
Quasar
Radio astronomy
Radio telescope
Red giant
Red shift
Royal Society
Satellite, artificial
Satellite, astronomical
Saturn
SI Units
Sirius
Solar energy
Solar System
Solar wind
Space exploration
Space medicine
Space probes
Space Shuttle
Space stations
Space telescope
Stars
Sun
Sunspots
Supernova
Telescope
Universe
Uranus
Van Allen belts
Variable stars
Venus
White dwarf
X-ray astronomy

Biographies

Archimedes
Aristarchus
Aristotle
Avogadro, Amedeo
Babbage, Charles
Baird, John Logie
Bell, Alexander
    Graham
Brahe, Tycho
Copernicus, Nicolaus
Curie, Marie and Pierre
Darwin, Charles
Davy, Sir Humphry
Descartes, René
Edison, Thomas Alva
Einstein, Albert
Faraday, Michael
Franklin, Benjamin
Freud, Sigmund
Galileo Galilei
Hero of Alexandria
Hippocrates
Kelvin, William
    Thomson
Kepler, Johannes
Lamarck, Jean Baptiste
Leonardo da Vinci
Linnaeus, Carolus
Marconi, Guglielmo
Morse, Samuel
Newton, Isaac
Nobel, Alfred
Planck, Max
Ptolemy
Rutherford, Ernest
Westinghouse, George

Chemistry

Acids and Bases
Aerosol
Alchemy
Alcohol
Alloy
Aluminium
Amalgam
Ammonia
Analysis, chemical
Anodizing
Antibiotics
Antifreeze
Antiseptics
Arsenic
Asbestos
Atom
Atomic number
Atomic weight
Barium
Battery
Benzene
Biochemistry
Bitumen
Bleaching
Boiling point
Bond, chemical
Brownian motion
Bunsen burner
Burning
Caffeine
Calcium
Carbon
Carbon dating
Carbon dioxide
Carbon fibres
Carbon monoxide
Cast iron
Catalyst
Caustic soda
Charcoal
Chemical reactions
Chemical symbols
Chemistry
Chlorine
Chlorofluorocarbons
    (CFCs)
Chlorophyll
Cholesterol
Chromatography
Chromium
Coal
Colloids
Combustion
Compound
Concentration
Condensation
Copper
Corrosion
Cracking
Crystals
Dehydration
Diffusion
Distillation
Drug
Dry ice
Ductility
Dyes
Electrolysis
Electron
Electroplating
Element, chemical
Emulsion
Epoxy resin
Evaporation
Experiment
Explosives
Fats
Fermentation
Fertilizers
Filtration
Fireworks
Flash point
Foam
Forensic science
Forging
Formula, chemical
Fossil fuels
Freezing point
Gas
Glycerol (Glycerine)
Gold
Gunpowder
Halogens
Hardness
Heavy water
Helium
Hydrocarbons
Hydrochloric acid
Hydrogen
Hydrogen bonds
Hydroxides
Hypertonic
Hypotonic
Ice
Indicator, chemical
Inorganic chemistry
Iodine
Ion
Iron and Steel
Isomer
Isotonic
Isotope
Kelvin (K)
Laboratory
Lactic acid
Laminates
Latent heat
Lead
Litmus
Magnesium
Malleability
Manganese
Margarine
Mass number
Mass spectroscopy
Melting point
Meniscus
Mercury
Metal fatigue
Metallurgy
Metals
Methane
Mixtures
Molecule
Natural gas
Neon
Neutron
Nickel
Nicotine
Nitrates
Nitric acid
Nitrogen
Nitroglycerine
Noble gases
Nylon
Octane
Oils
Organic chemistry
Osmosis
Oxidation and
    Reduction
Oxides
Oxygen
Ozone
Paint
Paraffin
Perfume
Periodic table
Petrochemicals
Petroleum
pH
Pharmacology
Phosphates
Phosphorus
Photochemistry
Pigments
Pitchblende
Plastics
Platinum
Plutonium
Poisons
Polymer
Positron
Potassium
Propane
Protein
Proton
Pyrex
Radioisotope
Radium
Royal Society
Rubber
Salt
Salts, chemical
Saturated solution
Semipermeable
    membrane
SI Units
Silicon
Silver
Soaps and Detergents
Sodium
Solute
Solution
Solvent
Spontaneous
    combustion
Stainless steel
Starch
States of matter
Steroids
Strontium
Sulphadrugs
Sulphates
Sulphides
Sulphur
Sulphur dioxide
Sulphuric acid
Suspension
Synthetic fibres
Tannin
Tin
Titanium
Titration
TNT
Trace elements
Tungsten
Uranium
Valency
Vapour
Vulcanizing
Water
Wax
Zinc

Earth Science

Acid rain
Air
Air pollution
Anemometer
Artesian well
Asbestos
Atmosphere
Aurora
Barometer
Bitumen
Cement
Chalk
Climate
Cloud
Coal
Colloids
Conservation,
    environmental
Continent
Cyclone
Deforestation
Desert
Desertification
Diamond
Earth
Earthquakes
Erosion and
    Weathering
Fertilizers
Fog
Fossil
Fossil fuels
Front, weather
Geography
Geology
Geomagnetism
Geothermal energy
Glacier
Greenhouse effect
Groundwater
Hard water
Hemisphere
Humidity
Hurricane
Hydrometer
Hygrometer
Ice
Ice Age
Igneous rocks
Ionosphere
Isobar
Isotherm
Jet stream
Landforms
Latitude and Longitude
Lava
Lightning
Lightning conductor
Map

Map projections
Metamorphic rocks
Meteorology
Mica
Minerals
Mining
Monsoon
Mountains
Natural gas
Nuclear waste
Ocean
Oils
Ore
Ozone layer
Plate tectonics
Poles
Pollution
Precipitation
Rainbow
Recycling
Resonance
Resources
Richter scale
Rivers and Lakes
Rocks
Sedimentary rocks
Seismograph
Soil
Stalactites and
  Stalagmites
Stratosphere
Theodolite
Thunder
Tidal power
Tidal waves and
  Tsunamis
Tides
Tornado
Tropics
Troposphere
Van Allen belts
Volcanoes
Waste disposal
Water
Water pollution
Water supply
Water table
Weather
Wind
Wind power

Electronics

Bar code
Bit and Byte
Calculator
Capacitor
Computer
Computer graphics
Computer languages
Computer memory
Digital
Diode
Electronics
Feedback
Filter, electronic
Hardware
Information technology
Integrated circuit
Language translation by
  computers
Logic
Microchip
Microprocessor
Modem
Rectifier
Robots
Semiconductor
Software
Speech recognition
Synthesizer
Transistor
Vacuum tube

Visual display unit
  (VDU)
Word processor

Life Science

Adaptation
Adolescence
Aging
Agriculture
AIDS
Allergy
Anatomy
Antenna
Antibiotics
Antibodies and Antigens
Antiseptics
Behaviour
Binocular vision
Biochemistry
Biological control
Biology
Bioluminescence
Biophysics
Biotechnology
Birth
Blood
Bone
Botany
Brain
Breathing
Breeding
Camouflage
Cancer
Carbohydrate
Carbon dioxide
Cell
Cell division
Cellulose
Cereals
Chlorophyll
Cholesterol
Chromosomes and
  Genes
Circulation
Classification
Clones
Conservation,
  environmental
Coordination
Cotyledon
Cytology
Dehydration
Dendrochronology
Digestion
Disease
Display
DNA
Dreams
Drug
Ear
Ecology
Ecosystem
Egg
Embryo
Endangered species
Environment
Enzymes
Evolution
Excretion
Experiment
Extinction
Eye
Fats
Feathers
Feedback
Feeding
Fermentation
Fertilization
Fertilizers
Fibres
Flowers
Food chain

Food poisoning
Forensic science
Fruit
Genetic engineering
Genetics
Gestation
Gills
Glands
Growth
Hair
Heart
Heredity
Hibernation
Homing
Hormone
Horticulture
Hybrid
Hydroponics
Hypothermia
Immune system
Infection
Instinct
Intelligence
Intestine
Joints
Kidneys
Laboratory
Lactic acid
Larva
Learning
Leaves
Liver
Lungs
Lymph system
Medicine
Memory
Metabolism
Metamorphosis
Microbiology
Microorganism
Migration
Milk
Monoclonal antibody
Movement and Motion
Muscle
Mutation
Natural selection
Nerves
Nicotine
Nose
Nucleic acid
Nucleus, cell
Nutrition
Oils
Organism
Osmosis
Pain
Paleontology
Pancreas
Parasite
Pasteurizaton
Pathology
Pesticides
Pharmacology
Photosynthesis
Physiology
Pigments
Plastic surgery
Poisons
Pollen and Pollination
Protein
Psychology and
  Psychiatry
Reflex
Reproduction
Respiration
Roots
Rubber
Seeds
Semipermeable
  membrane
Senses
SI Units

Skeleton
Skin
Sleep
Soil
Space medicine
Species
Speech
Starch
Stem
Sterilization
Steroids
Stomach
Streamlining
Sugars
Sulphadrugs
Symbiosis
Tannin
Taste
Teeth
Touch
Tranquillizers and
  Stimulants
Transpiration
Transplants
Vaccination
Veterinary medicine
Virus and Viral diseases
Vitamins
Water
Water supply
Wax
Wood
Yeast
Zoology
Zygote

Mathematics

Abacus
Algebra
Arithmetic
Average
Binary numbers
Decimal
Geometry
Graph
Infinity
Latitude and Longitude
Light year
Logic
Map
Map projections
Mass
Mathematics
Measurement
Metric system
Numbers
Optical character
  recognition
Oscillator
Polygon
Probability
Ratio
Rotation
Scales and Balances
Statistics
Symmetry
Weights and Measures

Physics

Absorption
Acceleration
Acoustics
Aerodynamics
Aerosol
Ampere
Antimatter
Atomic number
Atomic weight
Balancing point
Ballistics
Battery

Bimetallic strip
Bioluminescence
Biophysics
Black body
Boiling point
Brownian motion
Bubbles
Buoyancy
Capacitor
Capillary action
Carbon dating
Cathode ray tube
Celsius
Centre of gravity
Centrifugal force
Circuit, breaker
Circuit, electric
Cold
Colour
Compass
Condensation
Conduction, heat
Conductors, electric
Conservation
Contraction
Convection
Coulomb
Decibel
Density
Diffraction
Doppler effect
Echo
Efficiency
Elasticity
Electric arc
Electricity
Electromagnet
Electromagnetic radiatio
Energy
Entropy
Equilibrium
Escape velocity
Expansion
Experiment
Fahrenheit
Fallout, radioactive
Filter, electronic
Flotation
Fluid
Focus
Force
Foucault pendulum
Frequency
Friction
Fuse
Galvanometer
Gas
Generator, electric
Gravity
Gyrocompass
Gyroscope
Half-life
Hardness
Harmonics
Heat
Hertz
Hologram
Horsepower
Hydroelectricity
Hydrogen bomb
Hydrometer
Hygrometer
Implosion
Inductance, self and
  magnetic
Induction coil
Inertia
Inertial guidance
Infrared radiation
Insulation, thermal
Insulators, electrical
Iridescence
Joule

Joule's law
Kaleidoscope
Kelvin (K)
Kilowatt-hour
Laboratory
Laser
Latent heat
Lens, optical
Lever
Leyden jar
Light
Light year
Liquid
Liquid crystals
Lubrication
Luminescence
Mach number
Magdeburg spheres
Magnetism
Magnetometer
Magnification
Mass
Matter
Mechanics
Meniscus
Microwaves
Mirage
Mirror
Momentum
Movement and Motion
Music
Noise
Nuclear energy
Nuclear physics
Nuclear reactor
Nuclear waste
Oscillator
Oscilloscope
Parallax
Particle accelerator
Pendulum
Perpetual motion
Photoelectric cell
Photon
Physics
Piezoelectricity
Pneumatics
Polarized light
Positron
Power
Pressure
Prism
Quantum mechanics
Quantum theory
Radiation
Radioactivity
Rainbow
Red shift
Reflection
Refraction
Relativity
Resistance, electrical
Resonance
Revolution
Rotation
Royal Society
Saint Elmo's fire
SI Units
Solid
Sonar
Sound
Sound barrier
Space-time
Specific gravity
Specific heat capacity
Spectroscopy
Spectrum
Speech
Spontaneous
  combustion
States of matter
Static electricity
Steam

Stereoscope
Streamlining
Subatomic particles
Superconductor
Surface tension
Suspension
Temperature
Tensile strength
Terminal velocity
Thermocouple
Thermodynamics
Thermometer
Time
Torque
Torsion
Transformer
Ultra high frequency
  (UHF)
Ultrasound
Ultraviolet radiation
Vacuum
Vacuum flask
Van de Graaff
  generator
Vapour
Velocity
Very high frequency
  (VHF)
Viscosity
Volt
Watt
Wave
Wave motion
Wavelength
Weight
Work
X-ray astronomy
X-ray diffraction
X-rays

Technology

Abrasives
Adhesives
Aerosol
Air conditioning
Amplifier
Analogue
Anemometer
Anodizing
Antenna
Antifreeze
Aqualung
Arc lamp
Artificial intelligence
Automation
Balloon
Bar code
Battery
Bearings
Bimetallic strip
Biotechnology
Blast furnace
Bleaching
Body scanner
Camera
Canning
Carbon dating
Carbon fibres
Cassette recorder
Cast iron
Casting
Catalytic converter
Cellular radio and
  telephones
Cement
Centrifuge
Ceramics
CERN
Chromatography
Cinematography
Circuit breaker
Clocks and Watches

Communications
Compact disc player
Compass
Compressor
Construction
Cosmetics
Daguerreotype
Dehydration
Desalination
Diesel engine
Efficiency
Electric vehicle
Electrocardiograph
Electroencephalograph
Electron microscope
Electroscope, gold leaf
Engine
Extrusion
Fallout, radioactive
False-colour
  photography
Fax
Fibres, natural
Film, photographic
Fireworks
Flight
Flywheel
Foam rubber
Food additives
Food preservation
Forging
Foucault pendulum
Freeze-drying
Freezing
Fuel
Fuel cell
Fuel injection
Galvanizing
Gas turbine
Gears
Geiger counter
Genetic engineering
Glass
Governor
Gunpowder
Gyrocompass
Gyroscope
Gyrostabilizer
Heat exchanger
Heat pump
Heat shield
Heating systems
Hi-fi
Hologram
Homogenization
Horsepower
Hovercraft
Humidifier
Hydraulics
Hydroelectricity
Hydrofoil
Hydrometer
Hygrometer
Induction coil
Industrial revolution
Inertial guidance
Infrared photography
Injection moulding
Instruments, musical
Instruments, scientific
Internal-combustion
  engine
Invention
Ion propulsion
Irradiation
Irrigation
Jet propulsion
Kaleidoscope
Kiln
Laminates
Laser
Laser disc
Lathe

Lever
Light bulb
Light meter
Lighting, artificial
Lightning conductor
Linear motor
Liquid crystal display
  (LCD)
Locks and Keys
Loudspeaker
Lubrication
Machines, simple
Machine tools
Magnetic levitation
  (Maglev)
Magnetic tape
Magnetometer
Margarine
Maser
Mass spectroscopy
Materials
Mechanics
Metal detector
Metal fatigue
Meters, electricity and
  gas
Micrometer
Microphone
Microscope
Mining
Missiles
Motor, electric
Nuclear energy
Nylon
Octane
Oil refining
Optical character
  recognition
Optical fibres
Oscillator
Oscilloscope
Oxyacetylene welding
Paint
Paper
Paraffin
Particle accelerator
Pasteurization
Perfume
Petrochemicals
Petroleum
Photocopier
Photography
Pick-up
Pitchblende
Plastics
Pneumatics
Polaroid camera
Pottery and Porcelain
Printing
Pulley
Pump
Pyrex
Radar
Radio
Rangefinder
Records
Refrigeration
Revolution
Rockets
Rotation
Rubber
Safety glass
Satellite, artificial
Scales and Balances
Screws
Seismograph
Servomechanism
Siphon
Soaps and Detergents
Solar cell
Sonar
Sound recording
Space exploration

Space medicine
Space probes
Space Shuttle
Spectroscopy
Stainless steel
Steam engine
Stereophonic sound
Sterilization
Streamlining
Stroboscope
Submarine
Supersonic flight
Synthesizer
Synthetic fibres
Tape
Technology
Telecommunications
Telegraph
Telephone
Telescope
Television
Tempering
Tensile strength
Thermometer
Thermostat
Tidal power
Torque
Transistor
Tunnel
Turbine
Vacuum flask
Van de Graaff
  generator
Video camera
Video recorder
Visual display unit
  (VDU)
Vulcanizing
Wankel engine
Waste disposal
Water supply
Wave power
Welding
Wind power
Wind tunnel
Wire

Special Features Index

Agriculture
Air
Astronomy
Atom
Biology
Blood
Botany
Cell
Chemistry
Classification
Climate
Colour
Communications
Computer
Disease
Earth
Ecology
Electricity
Electronics

Energy
Evolution
Experiment
Flight
Flowers
Food chain
Fruit
Genetics
Geography
Geology

Heat
History of Science
Horticulture
Inorganic chemistry
Instruments, scientific
Landforms
Light
Magnetism
Mathematics
Measurement

Medicine
Meteorology
Microbiology
Movement and Motion
Nuclear physics
Numbers
Nutrition
Organic chemistry
Periodic table
Physics

Plastics
Pollution
Psychology and
 Psychiatry
Resources
Rocks
Seeds
SI Units
Soil
Solar System

Sound
Space exploration
Stars
Statistics
Steam engine
Technology
Veterinary medicine
Virus and Viral diseases
Water
Zoology

Acknowledgements

The publishers would like to thank the following artists for their contribution to this book:

Marion Appleton, Craig Austin, Kuo Kang Chen, David Eddington (Maggie Mundy Illustrator's Agency), Dave Etchell, Chris Forsey, Mark Franklin, Jeremy Gower, Hardlines, Hayward Art Group, Christa Hooke (Linden Artists), Lisa Horstman, Ian Howatson, Industrial Artists, Ian Jackson, John James (Temple Rogers), Felicity Kayes (Design Associates), Elly and Christopher King, Terence Lambert, Steve Latibeaudiere, Mike Long (Design Associates), Chris Lyon, Janos Marffy (Jillian Burgess Agency), William Oliver, David Phipps (Design Associates), Malcolm Porter, Sebastian Quigley (Linden Artists), John Ridyard, Valerie Sangster (Linden Artists), Mike Saunders (Jillian Burgess Agency), George Thompson, John Woodcock (Jillian Burgess Agency), David Wright (Jillian Burgess Agency).

The publishers wish to thank the following for supplying photographs for this book:

Cover Science Photo Library (SPL); page 1 SPL; 2 ZEFA; 5 VAG (UK) Ltd (top), Royal Albert Hall (bottom); 7 Paul Brierley; 9 ZEFA; 10 IVECO/Parlour Wood Ltd; 11 ZEFA; 12 SPL; 13 SPL; 15 ZEFA; 17 ZEFA; 18 Derby Museum & Art Gallery; 20 SPL; 21 McDonnell Douglas; 22 ZEFA; 23 SPL (left), ICI (right); 27 Ann Ronan Picture Library; 28 SPL; 29 SPL; 31 Ann Ronan Picture Library; 32 ZEFA; 34 Ronald Grant Archive; 36 Michael Holford (right), Paul Brierley (left); 37 Hutchison Library; 38 ZEFA; 39 SPL; 41 Istanbul University; 44 SPL (right), Grisewood & Dempsey (left); 45 ZEFA; 46 SPL; 48 ZEFA; 50 Science Museum; 51 Grisewood & Dempsey; 52 Mary Evans Picture Library; 53 ZEFA; 54 SPL; 58 ZEFA; 64 ZEFA; 65 SPL; 66 SPL; 67 Mansell Collection (top left), ZEFA (top right), Ann Ronan Picture Library (middle); 68 SPL; 71 F.R.Logan Ltd; 74 ZEFA; 75 SPL; 76 ZEFA (top), SPL (middle) 77 SPL; 78 SPL; 83 SPL; 84 SPL; 85 SPL; 87 ZEFA; 89 Robert Hunt Library (top), ZEFA (bottom); 95 Mike Potts (right), Beech Aircraft Corps (left); 96 Sony (UK) Ltd; 97 ZEFA; 103 Racal-Vodac Ltd; 104 SPL; 106 ZEFA; 108 D.Gardner (left), Isuzu Ceramics Institute (right); 110 SPL; 112 SPL; 115 Terry Cash; 116 Robert Hunt Library (right), ICI Chemicals & Polymers (left); 119 SPL; 120 Life Science Images; 121 SPL; 122 Lucas Film Ltd; 123 ZEFA; 131 ZEFA; 133 ZEFA; 135 NASA; 136 SPL; 139 Science Museum; 140 ZEFA (top), Atlas Copco (bottom); 141 The Moving Picture Co (top and left), Tektronik (UK) Ltd (right); 142 UNISYS; 143 Cray Research Inc; 146 ZEFA; 149 SPL; 151 Michael Hopkins & Partners; 152 ZEFA; 153 ZEFA; 154 ZEFA; 155 Ann Ronan Picture Library; 162 Popperfoto; 163 NASA; 165 National Museum of Photography, Film & Television; 166 Ann Ronan Picture Library (top), Michael Holford (bottom); 169 SPL; 170 SPL; 173 ZEFA; 175 De Beers (right), British Petroleum (left); 180 SPL; 181 ZEFA; 182 House of Seagram; 183 SPL; 185 Ann Ronan Picture Library; 186 SPL; 187 ZEFA; 191 NASA; 193 California Institute of Technology; 197 SPL; 198 Bettmann Archive; 200 PSA; 201 ZEFA; 203 ZEFA; 204 SPL; 209 Cambridge Instruments Ltd; 210 PSA (right), ZEFA (left); 212 Ron Boardman; 214 Herberts; 215 NHPA/M.Tweedie; 218 ZEFA; 220 Paul Brierley; 223 ZEFA; 224 ZEFA; 231 Byrne Photography (right), ZEFA (left); 236 Jet Propulsion Lab, Pasadena, California (left), SPL (right); 239 Canon (UK); 240 Bruce Coleman; 241 NHPA/S.Krasemann; 242 ZEFA; 244 SPL; 245 BTTG; 249 ZEFA; 251 ZEFA; 252 NHPA/D.Woodfall; 253 Ann Ronan Picture Library; 254 ZEFA; 255 ZEFA; 257 Ron Boardman; 259 SPL; 260 SPL; 262 FBI; 263 ZEFA; 264 Dinosaur National Museum, Utah; 265 Ron Boardman; 267 Novosti; 270 Ferodo/ADS Group; 271 SPL; 273 ZEFA; 276 ZEFA; 278 VAG (UK) Ltd; 284 SPL; 285 SPL; 291 SPL; 292 ZEFA; 293 ZEFA; 294 ZEFA; 295 ZEFA, 296 Johnson Matthey plc; 298 NASA; 307 ZEFA; 308 Bull HN Information Systems; 312 ZEFA; 313 Allsport; 314 SPL (left), Michael Holford (right); 316 ZEFA; 325 SPL; 326 ZEFA; 329 SPL; 330 ZEFA; 332 NASA; 334 ZEFA; 336 ZEFA; 337 ZEFA; 339 SPL; 341 ZEFA; 343 Nestlé; 344 ZEFA; 345 SPL; 350 Science Museum; 351 Transport Road & Research Laboratory; 352 SPL; 354 SPL; 355 ICI Group Ltd; 357 ZEFA; 358 Hutchison Library; 359 ZEFA (left), Photographic Services Corp (top), SPL (bottom); 360 NASA; 361 SPL; 362 ZEFA; 363 Shell Research Ltd; 365 Science Museum (top), SPL (bottom); 368 ZEFA; 369 SPL; 370 ZEFA; 373 British Gas plc; 374 MoD; 376 Ron Boardman; 382 ZEFA; 383 SPL; 385 Beech Aircraft Corps; 386 ZEFA; 387 ZEFA; 389 ZEFA; 390 NCR (left), ZEFA (right); 391 SPL; 393 Ron Boardman (left), ZEFA (right); 394 ZEFA; 400 ZEFA; 401 ZEFA; 402 ZEFA; 403 ZEFA (top), SPL (bottom); 406 Casio Electronics Ltd; 412 SPL; 417 British Airways; 418 Ann Ronan Picture Library; 419 SPL; 420 SPL; 422 SPL; 423 SPL; 428 NASA; 430 SPL (left), ZEFA (right); 432 Grisewood & Dempsey; 435 ZEFA; 437 SPL; 440 Biofotos (top), Ron Boardman (bottom); 441 SPL; 443 ZEFA; 444 SPL; 445 SPL; 448 Ron Boardman; 449 Hutchison Library; 450 ZEFA; 452 Ron Boardman; 453 SPL; 454 ZEFA; 459 ZEFA; 461 ZEFA; 463 ZEFA; 464 Spectrum Colour Library; 468 Grisewood & Dempsey; 469 Hutchison Library; 470 NASA; 473 ZEFA; 475 ZEFA; 478 SPL; 480 NHPA/M.Tweedie (top), SPL (bottom); 481 ZEFA; 484 ZEFA; 485 SPL (left), ZEFA (right); 487 Frank Lane Picture Agency; 489 ICI Explosives; 490 Nobel Foundation; 492 SPL; 494 SPL; 495 SPL; 496 ZEFA; 497 SPL; 501 SPL; 502 SPL; 503 ZEFA; 506 ZEFA; 508 SPL; 509 Ron Boardman; 510 SPL; 511 Science Museum; 512 Paul Brierly (top), SPL (bottom); 513 ZEFA; 514 SPL; 518 ICI Paints; 519 IMITOR; 520 The Hutchison Library; 529 SPL; 531 ICI Chemicals; 533 Ann Ronan Picture Library; 534 IMITOR; 535 Durst; 537 SPL; 541 Terry Cash; 542 SPL; 543 SPL; 544 SPL; 545 Ann Ronan Picture Library; 546 SPL; 547 SPL; 548 ICI Group; 549 ICI Group; 551 Johnson Matthey; 553 UK Atomic Energy Authority Technology; 555 SPL; 556 Polaroid UK; 557 SPL; 558 ZEFA; 559 Exxon Company USA (left), SPL (right); 562 ZEFA (left), SPL (right); 570 Calor Gas Ltd; 571 SPL; 572 Ann Ronan Picture Library (left), ZEFA (right); 573 Mansell Collection; 574 Derek Widdicombe; 575 Pyrex; 577 SPL; 578 SPL; 579 Marconi Co. Ltd; 581 ZEFA; 583 SPL; 585 Polygram; 590 Ann Ronan Picture Library; 591 NHPA/S.Dalton; 592 Frank Lane Picture Agency; 593 NHPA/A.Bannister; 594 ZEFA; 598 ZEFA; 599 ZEFA (top), National Film Archive (bottom), Hunter (left); 600 SPL; 604 Ann Ronan Picture Library (top), ZEFA (bottom); 606 ZEFA; 607 ZEFA; 611 NASA; 612 Science Museum; 613 Biofotos; 616 ZEFA; 619 Ron Boardman; 620 SPL; 621 SPL; 623 NHPA/A.Bannister; 624 ZEFA; 626 Derek Widdicombe; 627 SPL (top), D. Gardner (bottom); 629 ZEFA; 630 ZEFA; 633 SPL; 637 Marconi; 639 Ron Boardman; 641 ZEFA; 643 NASA; 644 NASA; 645 NASA; 647 SPL; 648 NASA; 652 NHPA/S.Krasemann; 653 SPL; 655 ZEFA; 659 Ron Boardman; 661 ZEFA; 663 NHPA/A.Bernard; 665 Ann Ronan Picture Library; 668 Frank Lane Picture Agency (right), SPL (left); 670 J. Allan Cash; 672 ZEFA; 673 Ron Boardman; 674 ZEFA; 675 SPL; 677 ZEFA; 679 ZEFA; 680 Ron Boardman; 681 Ron Boardman; 683 Yamaha; 684 Courtaulds Ltd; 685 ZEFA; 691 ZEFA; 692 ZEFA; 693 ZEFA; 694 ZEFA; 695 SPL (top), ZEFA (bottom); 696 ZEFA; 698 SPL; 699 ZEFA; 703 Ron Boardman; 705 ZEFA; 708 MAFF; 709 NHPA/S.Krasemann; 712 J. Allan Cash; 713 ZEFA; 714 ZEFA; 716 CEGB; 718 ZEFA (top), NHPA/G.Bernard (bottom); 720 SPL; 725 Ron Boardman; 726 Ontario Science Centre; 728 ZEFA; 729 SPL; 732 ZEFA (right), J. Allan Cash (left); 734 Sony UK; 735 SPL; 736 Samsung; 737 St. Bartholomew's Hospital; 738 ZEFA; 742 Genet Group; 743 NHPA/D.Woodfall; 744 ZEFA; 746 Panos Pictures; 749 SPL; 750 NHPA/S.Dalton; 753 Mark Edwards/Still Pictures (top), ZEFA (bottom); 755 Dennis Gilbert; 757 SPL (top), British Aerospace (bottom); 758 ZEFA; 761 Musée de l'air; 763 SPL (top), Grisewood & Dempsey (bottom); 764 SPL; 765 SPL; 766 Biofotos; 767 NHPA/M.Leach; 768 SPL.